Ordinary Guy

in

Extraordinary Times

Memoirs of a WWII Fighter Pilot

Lieutenant Colonel Robert H. McCampbell,
(Retired)

First Edition

SecondWind BookWorks

Ordinary Guy in Extraordinary Times

Memoirs of a WWII Fighter Pilot

By Lt. Colonel Robert H. McCampbell, (Retired)

Published by:
SecondWind BookWorks
Ventura, CA 93001
publisher@secondwindbookworks.com

ISBN 0-9771625-0-8

Library of Congress Catalog Card Number Pending
First Printing 2005
Printed in the United States of America

Acknowledgements

I gratefully appreciate the following individuals and organizations for providing photographs of aircraft and other areas of interest detailed in this manuscript. Without these references this book would not mean nearly as much to the reader.

Jesse Davidson Archives
Noorduyn, Inc
Nuovov Molise (Termoli, Italy newspaper)
Richard Bibb
U.S. Air Force
USAF Museum
U.S. Centennial of Flight
www.warbirdalley.com
www.warbirdsresourcegroup.org

Thank you for all the support my Ventura County Writers Club provided, especially James and Doris Vernon, Shlomo Kreitzer and Mario Speiser. Thanks to Lance Zedric, author and wordsmith.

Thanks to Jimmy McCauley, Ted Bullock, Frank Tribbett, and all the other Fourth Squadron buddies, who framed this unique experience. Here, I must acknowledge that the names of one or two of you have been changed for your protection from those vicious tabloids.

Thanks especially to Major James Wiley, who on the USSR shuttle mission, confirmed my ME109 aerial victory and gave me the most welcome and flattering newspaper recognition.

In thankful memory of Col. William A. "Bill" McCampbell, U.S. Army, Retired. You were my cousin, my lifetime mentor and chum, author and highly decorated leader of men on the final charge into western Germany.

Thanks to the relentless pressure to complete this book by my kids, Nancy, John, Mark and Kim.

And finally, thanks to Niles Cheney, without whose help this book might never have become more than a long-forgotten, messy manuscript.

Bob McCampbell
Ventura, California
2005

Dedication

To my beautiful, loving, compassionate, and care-giving wife and my pal for over 40 years. You have so gracefully allowed, encouraged and helped me to open this, an earlier chapter in my life. This was one preceding our incomparable union but certainly one that begged for a few, more-lasting, written impressions of extraordinary times. Further, likened to the "September Song", opportunities for doing so were dwindling "down to a precious few." You have given me so much and now I must thank you for even another ... for holding my hand through the misty wilderness of the past toward the welcome catharsis that is fed by these memoirs.

Bob McCampbell
Ventura, California
2005

Disclaimer

These are the memories of Bob McCampbell as he recalls them after 60 years. Dates, places and people noted herein are from the notes and memory of the author.

Merriam-Webster's Unabridged dictionary defines *memoirs* as: "an autobiographical account often anecdotal or intimate in tone whose focus of attention is usually on the persons, events, or times known to the writer."

Any discrepancies you may find are unintentional and the author apologizes for inaccuracies.

Enjoy his "extraordinary times" ...

The Publisher

SecondWind BookWorks

Contents

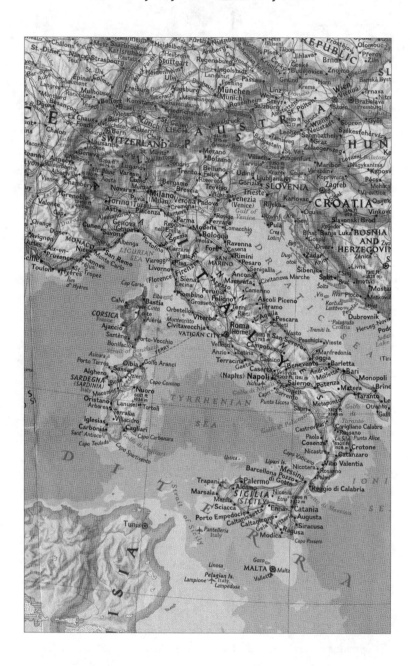

Illustrations

Preface

Through the years I repeatedly urged my Dad to render a sketch of his remarkably interesting life. I hoped for some lingering recounts of his life pre-me and his early 20th Century youth.

As a boy I coveted my Dad's occasional anecdotes of his WWI experiences. Couldn't I at least capture those in ink? No, it never happened. So, as I suffered through a recent round of my kids' nagging at me to do the same, I could make no more excuses.

Many of the wartime events covered in these memoirs I told to my kids as they were growing up. I am sure you will understand that in the interest of avoiding disillusionment in young minds, the versions I told them may have been more the stuff of image preservation. So, Nancy, John, Mark and Kim, now that you have discovered your dad was not perfect after all, perhaps like the Santa Claus thing, you'll be able to tolerate the apparent historical revisionism lurking in these memoirs.

It is my sincere hope that my advanced maturity now has allowed me to reflect and report more accurately the feelings, fears, and foolhardy stuff of a rather average young World War II fighter pilot. In so doing, I may be risking an image betrayal of the cocky, devil-may-care stereotype.

Fighter pilots, like all human beings, differed widely in personalities. On the other hand, our rather specialized career field nurtured some common traits. We each took great pride in our membership in the fighter pilot fraternity. This alone generated strong camaraderie. As a spin-off, a boost in self-confidence followed. A more complex emotion, apparently common to all warriors, was fear. Since military flying was a risky business, with or without an adversary, fear was our constant companion.

Fear was a closet devil, rarely discussed or shown. Some of us eventually realized that openly acknowledging fear diluted its effects. It was certainly handled differently by each man. As you know, the stereotype pilot, with his nerves of steel, never felt fear. Personally, I failed to run across any seasoned heroes or fledglings who considered fear uncommon. Some, somehow, just managed it better than others.

We were all glad to embrace the belief that pilots were great lovers! Perhaps Freud would have explained this arrogant fantasy as one derived from the pilot's metaphorical dream that the fighter plane embodied the ultimate, indomitable phallic symbol. Move over Sigmund!

It cannot be denied that there were, in most battle-tested fighter outfits, a few admirable standout warriors. These were the rare birds who clearly showed more finely honed skills, aggressiveness, confidence and achievements than most. I doubt many of these would have passed the full criteria of the stereotype test.

But, whatever the case, we average fighter pilots, by definition, were in the majority. At the risk of a humility lapse, I'm convinced that our cumulative log bulges with experiences begging to be unwrapped. Dredged up in these memoirs are some samples. You be the judge.

***We were ordinary guys living through
some extraordinary times.***

Chapter 1

How'd I Get Here?

"Tackle Red One, Yellow One here. Yellow Four dragging rough engine, wants abort ... OK?"

"Yellow One from Red One, uh ... OK Yellow Four, abort alone ... Out"

Damn it! I'm already short two!

This was to be my first go as squadron leader and I was hoping for all the help I could get. I was leading thirteen P–51 Mustang fighter planes toward a planned rendezvous with a sky-full of B–24 heavy bombers. Those guys would be looking to us for protection from enemy fighters and I didn't want to disappoint them.

It was summer of 1944, in the skies over Southern Europe. As we climbed northward, edging the Italian Adriatic coast, it was impossible to ignore the striking scenic contrasts. The remarkable beauty of the shoreline, the northern Italian cities and lakes, and now thrusting skyward, the majestic snow-capped Alpine peaks. All were compelling distractions. Moreover, at above 20,000 feet these landmarks were so clearly identifiable that navigation was a cinch. A few scattered high clouds accentuated the scene. My mind drifted.

Was I actually leading a fighter squadron on a world war combat mission over Europe? How did I ever end up here? And why me?

"Flak burst, nine o'clock low!" crackled in my earphones and brought me back to reality. I was at war!

Daydreams had been an overused escape mechanism in my pre-war youth. Here's how I got from daydreams to World War Two.

Chapter 2

Perils of Pylons, Puberty and Poland

Growing Pains—1934

With the exception of Los Angeles, Southern California was rather sparsely populated in 1934. The endless summer of my carefree childhood was ending. Fleeting were the magic days of adventuring with my neighborhood buddies through the then-unspoiled, lush Ventura River environs. Put away the slingshots, the home-built pirate rafts on the pond, and the irreverent bare-bottom frolicking in the swimming holes. I was bussed from my semi-rural Ventura Avenue home to attend Cabrillo Junior High School. This was the biggest institution I could imagine and it schooled Ventura's seventh through tenth graders.

At age eleven I was younger than most seventh graders and going on ahead of my neighborhood chums. I felt overwhelmed and lost in a sea of more physically and mentally mature kids. But worse yet, family life was in disarray. Sadly, my parents had forgotten their marriage vows. My Dad had managed to hold a good job in the thirties, allowing us some enjoyable summer vacations and other perks. Through his steady oil refinery income of about $200 per month, our family had pretty much dodged the widespread miseries of the Depression. So, the trauma of my parents split-up was compounded by its impact on the family finances. I was nursing the consequences of this entire tragedy via my lonely perspective as a non-sibling. How could my perfect family so self-destruct?

Even though I was an undersized, under-motivated kid of scant means, new friends at school seemed to compensate for life's other shortcomings. Gordon Kimball, a junior high classmate, became my first close non-neighborhood buddy. In contrast to me, Gordon was a real achiever and a member of a highly respected old ranching family in nearby Saticoy. He was about my size, certainly likable and we shared common interests. I met Gordon on the junior high tennis courts ... and here I must back up a little.

Mom's Great Gift

At age 10 I had received the gift of a lifetime although I didn't know it then. Despite my initial resistance, my incredible mother dragged me out on some nearby courts and taught me the basics of tennis. I still love the game and play regularly. My mother's gift was passed along to my wife, our children and grandchildren. Two of our four kids are tennis professionals. The others love the game.

Through friends like Gordon, my junior high days rapidly became more rewarding. A long-time interest in airplane model building was being nudged aside by interests in more socially interactive things like competitive tennis, ocean sports and just being a teen. As to ocean sports, I should mention that we had no surfboards at that time and a big local fad was surf riding on kayaks and body surfing. Gordon had a couple of kayaks at the family beach cottage and got me started.

Fertile Flying Field—Mines Field—1936

My Dad rekindled the flame of my long-time fascination with aviation by taking me to the 1936 National Air Races. The event was held that year at Mines Field, better known today as Los Angeles International Airport, or LAX. It amounted to a vast rural grassland with a few small hangers. Its perimeter had been newly fenced; probably as a barrier to the livestock and other potential gatecrashers.

Maybe it was just me, but as we parked and jumped out of the car I thought I could feel the vibes of universal excitement from the crowd. I was spellbound as I approached, and even touched, some of the racing planes that had inspired me from my flying magazines and books. Right there was the famous, stocky, cylinder-shaped *GB Sportster* which had carried Jimmy Doolittle to victory in the 1932 closed circuit Thompson Trophy Race. Sadly, this race had also carried several well-known racing pilots on their final quests to slip the surly bonds of earth. Resting nearby was Benny Howard's *Mister Mulligan*, the 1935 winner of both the Thompson Trophy pylon race and the Los Angeles to New York Bendix Race.

Wedell-Williams Special Racer
and Roscoe Turner
Photo courtesy of U.S. Centennial of Flight

But more exciting, standing alongside his *Wedell-Williams Special Racer*, and not twenty feet away, was the world-famous aviator, Roscoe Turner. Here he posed, surrounded by fans and press. Turner was the consummate showman, with his sky blue

Roscoe Turner with Thompson Trophy
Photo courtesy of U.S. Centennial of Flight

blazer, tan breeches and riding boots. Roscoe more than lived up to his billing. When I saw him, he was well known as a winner of the Thompson (later he would win two more). He was famous for many other flying feats and records as well. In retrospect, this was in spite of the probable drag imposed by his classic handlebar mustache and big toothy smile. The media coverage showered upon such aviators was substantial and elevated them to the celebrity stature of the great athletes and movie stars of the day.

The annual National Air Races became the premier aviation event held in the United States prior to WWII. The show included aerobatics performances, Army and Navy air demonstrations, competitions and some thrilling exhibitions by foreign military pilots. But the show-stopper, and international attention getter each year, was the closed circuit Thompson Trophy Race. The Thompson that I watched certainly captured and enraptured my 13-year-old attention.

Adding to my unique fascination was the participation in the Thompson of a local Ventura flyer, Marion McKeen, who was a friend of my Dad's. The only taint on this memory was that at age five I had been too frightened to accept McKeen's offer of a flight in his colorful biplane. It still haunts me. Unfortunately, McKeen and his *City of Los Angeles* were forced out in mid-race with an engine malfunction. He did go on to win other air races of national prominence.

As the racers screamed past the grandstand, I was sure I could see the strained faces of those daring pilots as they whipped their chariots for more speed. Here they were nudging the ground and the limits of those engines toward a shuttering turn round the pylon nearest the grandstands. Through the years, the Thompson had been an infamous widow maker. There were close calls this time, with engine failures and other near misses, but luckily, no fatalities.

The 1936 Thompson race did end in some unusual excitement, actually international in substance. Unhappily, its outcome proved a discouraging one for U.S. pilots and fans. The event was won by a French pilot, Michel Detroyat, in his sleek, yellow, low-winged, *Caudron Racer*. Detroyat's speed deed was done in record time, covering the course with an unheard of dash of over 300 mph. His speedster was reportedly developed with a subsidy from the French government.

Roscoe Turner reflected the bitterness of the also-ran U.S. pilots saying, "It just isn't fair for a foreign government to trim a bunch of little guys who build airplanes in their backyards." Perhaps so, but Roscoe himself was helped appreciably by big money sponsors. Anyway, it seems doubtful to me that any pilot of that era would have doggedly pursued a similar

American subsidy. The planes of the 1936 U.S. military could hardly keep up with the backyard racers.

How could I have dreamed that in less than a decade I would be flying far speedier, more powerful, reliable and versatile airplanes than any of those cutting edge racers. Even more remarkable is the fact that the WWII vintage fighter planes have continued to dominate the Thompson Trophy Race ever since WWII. All, of course, were ordered by and produced for the U.S. military, albeit later enhanced as racing planes with some tinkering by the more recent American backyard pilots.

Santa Barbara—1937

In the mid-summer of 1937 Mom took a secretarial job at the Santa Barbara County Probation Department. My concerns of missing my former Ventura buddies healed pretty fast. With her starting salary of $80 a month we moved into a $25 per month two-bedroom stucco near the beach and municipal tennis courts. New friends abounded in these idyllic surroundings.

I enrolled in the Santa Barbara High School's tenth grade and brought with me only one general problem. At age fourteen I was 5 feet tall and weighed 100 pounds. Although I had always enjoyed playing all sports it was obvious; I wasn't going to letter in football or basketball. I did make the tennis team and the sport was strong at Santa Barbara High. The sport also opened a bundle of friendships and gave me some confidence, which I needed in the worst way.

My most memorable tennis moment occurred in high school in the 1939 California Interscholastic Federation playoffs. It was the semifinals against Montebello High, in a Los Angeles suburb. Jack Kramer, one of the all-time greats and the then top U.S. junior player, filled the number one spot for Montebello. His coach decided that since they had two other top-ranked players but were weak down the line, he would play Kramer at second doubles paired with their weakest team member. The strategy, of course, was that Kramer could easily carry the doubles playing with anybody and that Montebello was strong enough in singles without Kramer. Bob Wormser, our coach, surprisingly responded in kind. He placed our #1, Tom Kruger, and our bottom man, me, as a doubles team.

Fittingly, Santa Barbara and Montebello were even at the wire. Then it happened. Kruger and I beat Kramer and his partner in straight sets. To this day I enjoy telling folks about the time I beat Jack Kramer, who went on to become an international tennis legend. Actually, it was Tom Kruger who had played great. I played well for me, but Jack Kramer's partner was too much of an anchor ... even for him.

High school years got progressively better for me as I began to grow physically. Girls began to pay some attention and who wouldn't be happy living in the beautiful sunny Santa Barbara environment? But, one always wants more ... you guessed it ... money! That kind of greed got me a depression job at one dollar a day and room and board at a multimillionaire's citrus ranch about 150 miles distant in Covina, California. This kept me off the streets during the summer vacation between my junior and senior years of high school. It also gave me a defining moment of maturation while milking the cow early one September 1939 morning.

Milking was the first and last chore of a hard 12-hour day of doing everything from driving a tractor to cleaning the swimming pool. Those quiet hours with "Old Bossy" were sweetened by dance band music from my small barnyard radio. Just a few days before returning to my final high school year my music program and my milking rhythm were interrupted by a news special. Hitler's Nazi Germany had invaded

Poland. England and France, in turn and by treaty, had declared war on Germany. Tragically, the short fuse of World War II had ignited. The message of potential impact on our country and particularly on people my age was not lost. Even at sixteen, I knew this dramatic and sudden event would hasten my journey to manhood.

Chapter 3

Found: Higher Education Than College

Sad Grad—June 1940

The war situation during my 1940 senior high school year demands a glance. Relative to the September 1939 invasion of Poland, Hitler's surprisingly efficient war machine crushed all organized Polish resistance in a matter of days.

England and France were jointly reluctant to intervene; their mutual defense treaty with Poland amounted to little ... Especially for the Poles. The matter did remain that three major world powers, England, France and Germany, were officially at war. England and France readied themselves first to defend France against a German invasion. As it turned out they would have almost nine months to prepare. The French relied greatly on their impenetrable Maginot Line bordering Germany. The Brits brought across several hundred thousand ground troops and equipment as well as a number of fighter and light bomber squadrons. The British were principally manning the northwestern French borders beyond the reaches of the Maginot Line.

A so-called "Phony War" had ensued on the Western European Front spanning most of my senior year in high school. Propaganda leaflets scattered from opposing planes and cannon seemed to constitute the major war effort. We, and much of the rest of the world, were lulled into a mind-set of "What War?" In May of 1940 our complacency was shattered. A sudden, massive, coordinated German attack exploded southward. It was spearheaded with lightening-speed and precision by air and land forces through Belgium and the Netherlands toward France. It was developing momentum into a giant pincer movement and was completely bypassing the impregnable Maginot Line. The novel military maneuver was soon to be heralded world-wide as the "Blitzkrieg" or Lightening War. It quickly spread a myth of Nazi invulnerability.

I was practicing for my high school graduation when the school broadcast a bulletin announcing the fall of France to the Germans. It was June 1940. My fellow graduates and I were shocked with feelings shared across a stunned world; How could France, a traditional ally, a major world power itself and one bolstered by the complete military support of Great Britain, be overwhelmed in little more than a month's time? Without a doubt the British will soon be kicked off the continent. What next?

Since I had not been an outstanding student or a star athlete at Santa Barbara High School, my college prospects didn't look very good. Late in my senior year the school principal interviewed me while reviewing my grades.

"Bob, what are you planning to do in the future?"

"Well, sir, I'm planning to go on to college."

He cleared his throat nervously, "Uh ... Bob, I really don't think you ought to try that. You have a nice personality, so, let's talk about some other directions we might take ... something for which you might be better suited."

Despite my principal's doubts, I squeezed into Santa Barbara State College, today the University of California, Santa Barbara, and passed my first semester. I was pledged into a fraternity by the second semester and endured almost as much hell during initiation as I did later in the war. My high school tennis experience prompted the coach to recruit me for the college tennis team. The season started out slowly, but we turned it around and recorded wins over San Jose State, Fresno State, and San Diego State to win the California College Athletic Association Championship.

Completing my freshman college year with better grades than I made in high school proved that maybe I knew more than my old high school principal about my potential! I was feeling good about my freshman year at SBSC, but I had also graduated to the ripe old age of 18 and was now eligible for the newly established military draft.

I took a summer job in a large chain variety store in Santa Barbara and instead of returning to fall college as a sophomore. I accepted a pay raise and enrollment in the chain's management training program. Twenty-five bucks a week was big money!

One day, while in the throes of wondering about my decision, a college friend showed me some sample math questions from the U.S. Army Air Corps Aviation Cadet entrance exam.

Military service had been a hot topic of discussion during my freshman year at SBSC and my appetite was whetted when my friend suggested applying for aviation cadet training.

I had wanted to be a pilot from childhood, but these samples pretty well convinced me that only a miracle would get me through the math portion of the exam. But my friend was similarly concerned and invited me to join him in some refresher math studies to be conducted by his cousin, a math whiz.

So, in the sunset weeks of the fall evenings of 1941 we sat with the whiz in his gas company boiler room getting up steam to tackle the exam's math problems. I felt I was cramming for the most important exam of my life.

The War Becomes Our War—1941

Unbeknownst to its citizens and apparently to its military, the U.S. was about to face one of the biggest exams of its life. England and the USSR were the last remaining holdouts against a Nazi takeover of Europe. In Asia, the Empire of Japan was belligerently expanding. President Roosevelt had long recognized the world dilemma and pursued some American defense preparedness initiatives. Through controversial legal maneuvers, Roosevelt had even successfully provided some military and other assistance to the embattled forces of Great Britain, France and China, but not without taking loud criticism at home.

A major roadblock to a military build-up in the U.S. came in the form of a strong national isolationist movement. Its leaders, including national hero, Colonel Charles A. Lindberg, railed against U.S. participation in any kind of cooperative international involvement and especially military alliances. Isolationism had gathered political momentum. We could simply stay out of foreign wars.

Almost inevitably, on December 7, 1941, as I was wondering if I'd learned enough math, the event happened. The Empire of Japan preemptively struck U.S. military bases in Hawaii, inflicting the most devastating destruction of military lives and resources we could imagine in a single attack. Ironically, by the attack's very nature, an unforeseeable force was awakened in sleepy America, which would lead to Japan's eventual downfall. The mood of the nation would probably never again change so dramatically as it did that day. Isolationism died an instant death. It's doubtful that ever again could our nation rally with such durable oneness of purpose and accomplishment.

Obstacle Curse

The first obstacle in my naïve quest for glory in the wartime skies was my age. I had to be twenty-one to apply for Army Air Corps or Navy flight training. A recruiting sergeant advised me that all I had to do was to join the Army and then submit my application to the Air Corps, then my age would be no problem. Had I followed his advice, the only propeller I would have seen would have been from an enemy plane shooting at me in the trenches.

I had intended to follow the recruiter's direction, but as I was getting into the car to drive to the recruiting office in Ventura, a neighbor greeted me from her front lawn.

"Hey, Bobby," she called. "I see here they've lowered the age limit for flying cadets to eighteen. Is that what you're gonna sign up for?"

"You see what?" I exclaimed, as I ran over to see for myself.

I soon headed north to the nearest flying cadet application and testing facility. It was Hancock Field, the Air Corps Primary Flying School in Santa Maria, California.

Having had one year of college got me in the door. It was a long process of testing. The written and physical portions took two days each and I got the test results by the evening of the second day. Whatever I said at the time, It was an understated feeling of gratification when I learned that I'd passed and that I was scheduled for the physical the next morning.

The next obstacle was weight or a lack of it. At five feet ten inches and 125 pounds, I was underweight by a couple of pounds. A fellow applicant suggested that I stuff myself with all the bananas and water I could hold. With a terrible stomachache, I barely edged the minimum.

During the next battery, the doctor asked,

"Have you been ill lately?

To which I replied with tongue in cheek, "Well, yes sir. I just got over the flu."

The doctor scheduled a retest for the following morning. "On the whole physical?" I asked,

"No, not on the stuff you've already passed."

I returned the next day and passed the vital signs physical with flying colors. Voila! I was a flying cadet! Bananas and water made the difference between becoming an aviation cadet and an infantry buck private!

Preflight Blight—Williams Army Airfield

The aviation cadet application, screening and acceptance process lasted from mid-December 1941 well into January 1942. By late January, I had orders and was on a train with an old school friend, Dominic Perello, headed for Williams Army Airfield, Arizona. We were among the first post-hostilities groups to be sent for pre-flight training.

And were things screwed up ... no uniforms! Since no one in charge seemed to know what to do with us we spent most of our days drilling in civilian clothes, in the Arizona desert. We did have a few classroom briefings on military discipline, courtesy and an occasional morale film.

Within a week we were issued coveralls, and soon got a shipment of World War I Springfield rifles crated in Cosmoline. We were each issued a rifle, buried in this grease since the first world war. We were ordered to clean our weapons for inspection the following day. What an impossible mess! From a distance we looked with envy at some flying cadets going to and from their airplanes and wondered if we'd ever get to that point.

Empire of Japan Declares War on Santa Barbara

While suffering one evening from barracks-boredom, we heard a radio news flash that a Japanese naval force shelled Santa Barbara. I had visions of mass destruction, heavy casualties and chaos. Dominic and I tried to call home but to no avail. Hours later we learned that a Japanese submarine had surfaced about fifteen miles up the coast from Santa Barbara and lobbed several shells from its deck cannon into an abandoned oil field. Nobody hurt, no real damage done, but the incident certainly brought the war home. In later months, an enterprising local humorist produced bumper stickers reading, "AVENGE ELWOOD!" which was the name of a small truck stop and oil fields nearest to the area "devastated."

In mid-February we were moved to the newly constructed Santa Ana Army Air Base in Santa Ana, California, established to indoctrinate, process and billet aviation cadets. Here we had reasonable and pertinent classroom and physical training but also more obstacles. We had all understood that our initial screening tests had cleared our way to pilot training, but now a new battery of tests was given to sort out those best suited for pilot or bombardier or navigator training. For some unknown reason I was sorted, happily, into the pilot bin.

Cal Aero Flight Academy, Ontario, California

From here things moved fast and by early March 1942, I found myself in Cal Aero Flight Academy, Ontario, California. This pre-war contract flying school, now administered by the Army, was about 50 miles of orange groves east of Los Angeles. It still had civilian instructors with military check pilots conducting evaluations of each cadet. The planes were Stearman PT–13s; sturdy, forgiving, open cockpit biplanes.

Most of the other cadets in my class had experienced some preliminary flight training in federally sponsored college programs. I'd had none, so at the start was more disoriented in the air than most.

Cal Aero Flight Academy
Photo courtesy of Bob McCampbell

Actually, I narrowly avoided washing out of the flying program within the first few hours of training. Contrary to childhood glory dreams, being airborne took some getting used to. I didn't see how I was going to meet the requirement that a cadet be ready to solo within eight hours of instruction.

My initial instructor was a loud, ass-chewing, Pavlovian molder of men. He regularly whipped the stick from my hands to show displeasure. I could only show mine by doing a poor job of flying. My eight-hour quota was dwindling down to a precious few minutes when a miracle happened. Can't say why or how, but suddenly I was assigned to another instructor.

Mr. Smith was a quiet-spoken, smiling, easy going guy in his early thirties. After one ride under my new mentor's relaxed tutelage I was gaining confidence. On the next ride, he asked me to land and, with a broader than usual grin, he jumped out of the plane as it rolled to a stop. There I sat, feeling really naked and alone in the cockpit. Smith pointed to me with one hand and to the sky with the other.

Now or Never

Before I knew it, I taxied back to the start of the runway. With a deep breath, I shoved on the throttle and danced on the rudder pedals to keep the thing straight. Then, oh yes, stick forward, to raise the tail. Next, I eased back on the stick and headed skyward.

"What God-forsaken reason," I wondered, "was I doing up here alone?"

A sweaty palm somehow guided the Stearman around the flight pattern, eased it back down and settled it on the grass, with a slight bounce. Smith's smile wasn't too hard for me to mirror as he greeted my landing with two thumbs up. I was ecstatic!

The ground classes were tough too. A bundle of stuff such as navigation, meteorology, general aeronautics and military protocol were laid on us with homework and little time for study. Even tougher was the upper class hazing system that controlled our lives from reveille to taps. There was one welcome exception: no hazing permitted on the flight line. Studying around the flight line was better than no study at all. Theoretically we were eligible for leave on most weekends. Unfortunately, the upper-classmen made certain

First Trainer - Boeing/Stearman PT - 13
Photo courtesy of WarbirdAlley.com

each of us Jackpots, as we primary fledglings were called, collected enough demerits to deny eligibility for a gate pass.

Flying, nonetheless, became increasingly more rewarding. Mr. Smith steadfastly but reassuringly instructed us day by day in new maneuvers and techniques and turned us loose to practice them. Gradually, my primary training was culminating in a pleasing new note of confidence and achievement. But the day arrived when one last hurdle sent the anxiety altimeter soaring. It was the inescapable, foreboding check ride with an Army check pilot. This test would either send me on to basic flying school or to some oblivious, square one, Army duty.

Check Mate

Lieutenant Whitehorse, a swarthy, well-proportioned, no-nonsense Sioux Indian met me as scheduled at the flight line. The man was God. He held in his hands everything of importance in my life.

I rendered my best salute. He returned it and ordered me into an awaiting Stearman. The lieutenant jumped into the rear cockpit and advised me to take off and climb to 4,000 feet. It always seemed to take forever to climb the Stearman to that altitude. Now I was getting there much too soon and Whitehorse, without pause, began the ritual.

"OK Mister, let me see some lazy eights"

I did some and then he started me through the rest of required maneuvers. I did a sloppy job. He cut the power and shouted, "Forced landing!"

The procedure is to head without power to the nearest and best emergency spot and almost touch down. I wound up heading for some high-tension wires. He jammed the throttle open at the last second and pulled the plane up over the wires. After directing me through some other tasks, he demanded, "Let's see a slow roll."

A slow roll requires rolling the airplane around its own axis until upright again. This should be accomplished without losing altitude or direction. It necessitates well-coordinated use of stick and rudder controls. While rolling around toward the upside-down position, the pilot must push the stick forward to keep the nose up and avoid falling out or downward.

In the case at hand, I fell out of the roll. Whitehorse again challenged me to a forced landing.

This time what looked to me like a pretty smooth pasture turned out to be a vineyard. Whitehorse grabbed the controls again. My scalp had a temporary feeling.

Smith's Thumbs Always Up

My instructor, Mr. Smith, was understandably disappointed when advised of my thumbs down checkride. He insisted I could fly better and that the system did allow for one more final military check ride. So he confidently smiled and said, "Mac, grab your stuff and let's you and me go bore some holes in the sky."

Away we flew ... through the routine with Smith's reassuring guidance. When we landed I thought, *God, Why couldn't I have flown like that for Whitehorse?*

"Mac you can do it, you're a good pilot," said Smith. "If it helps any, think of me in your back seat when you fly with the check pilot tomorrow."

Following a rather sleepless night, fraught with feelings akin to ... hey, my whole life is on the line! I rose and with a less-than steady hand, shaved, showered and caught a bite of breakfast. Waiting for me at the flight line was the scalper, Lieutenant Whitehorse. Miraculously, a daydream took over and there was Mr. Smith in the lieutenant's garb jumping in the rear cockpit. My hands steadied and my confidence lifted as I flew the prescribed course on automatic, a smooth slow roll, a perfect spin recovery, a well executed line-up on a smooth meadow for a forced landing.

I had heard no discouraging words from Whitehorse in the process. Still, the whole up-beat dream began to mist as I shot what I felt was an OK three point landing. The unbearable, unsteady feeling was re-emerging as we dismounted the Stearman. There stood the real Lieutenant Whitehorse.

"Mr. McCampbell, good ride. Why the hell didn't you fly like that the first time?"

Couldn't have said it better myself! Thank you, thank you, Mr. Smith!

That evening Mr. Smith drove the five of us, his students, to a local restaurant to celebrate our graduation from primary. I didn't know if he had got the word that I had passed my check ride. It just so happened it was driving him crazy but he just couldn't bring himself to ask. Then Jennings, a fellow cadet who did know, suddenly offered, "How about it Sir? You got all of us through ... even Mac!" To which Mr. Smith's heretofore worried face brightens and begs, "No kidding?"

Primary Flight Training Class
Jennings, Cottrell, McCampbell, Amos, Smith, Anderson
Photo courtesy of Bob McCampbell

Further, the man of never a word of profanity, nor a show of wild emotionality, stops the car and threads his arm between his two front seat passengers. With a handshake for me, he shouts, "God damned Mac, you did it? Whoooo-eeee!!!"

Bye-Bye Biplane

So, after a little more than two months of primary training in the PTs, those who passed the Army check pilot's final terrorizing ride were promoted to basic flight training. Luckily for us, Cal Aero was one of the only flying schools that included both primary and basic flight training at the same location. Also we felt grateful not to be among the more than 50% of the primary trainees in the class who had washed out.

Now we were upper-classmen. However, after a few days of throwing our weight around amongst the newly arrived primary jackpots, the Army abolished the hazing system. Considering the multitude of wartime exigencies and priorities, hazing missed the cut on the must-do list. Basic did allow us a much more relaxed life including time off base on weekends.

Hundreds of flight training schools were blossoming across the country, especially in the Southwest with its weather advantage. Our basic trainer was a Vultee BT–13, a heavy, low wing, 2-seat, noisy, fixed landing gear, radial engine, clumsy flying thing. We called the plane the Vultee Vibrator. We were restricted from doing the aerobatics in the BT that we had learned and loved so much in the Stearman. Looking back it seems we could have used that basic time more profitably in an airplane capable of simulating combat gymnastics. At any rate we did get some valued instrument and navigational time as well as experience in handling single wing planes with heavier wing loadings.

Basic Trainer - Vultee BT – 13
Photo courtesy of WarbirdAlley.com

I missed my old instructor from primary who had been a strong, yet reassuring teacher. My new civilian flight instructor was not a great mentor and besides was nervous as hell. He almost got us lost on a night navigational flight. I was glad to have prevailed in a navigational disagreement in the night sky over the Mojave Desert. I did have the advantage of a familiarity with the southern California cities and topography. Now I see how difficult it must have been for the Army to recruit instructors who had flown anything beyond a light plane. In many instances, during these early days of the war, student and instructor were struggling up the same learning curve.

Basically Beswitched

My flying progress through basic training was adequate and I passed the military mid-term check ride. An occasional losing bout with an absent mind gave me a few close calls throughout my training. One such occasion came close, once again, to washing me out of the cadet program. It happened as I turned on a final landing approach.

Surprisingly, I had found myself cut off by another cadet squeezing in dangerously close ahead. I don't think he saw me. With a profanity, I gunned the engine and pulled up to go around for another try. New surprise! My engine coughed and screamed the thunderous sound of silence and the quiet sight of a stilled propeller. I was at maybe 200 feet over mid-runway. Nothing to do but to try and squeeze into what landing area remained straight ahead. With full flaps and some side-slipping to reduce speed, I managed to touch down, unbent, toward the runway's end. I stopped in the rough and just short of the fence.

With an exhalation of relief, I was actually anticipating some congratulations on my emergency landing skills. Then the crash truck rolled up with a mechanic and the senior flight instructor aboard.

"What happened?" asked the instructor.

"Well," I replied. "A guy cut me off on final ... tried to go around ... the engine quit."

As I dismounted, they climbed up on each side of the cockpit. The mechanic tried unsuccessfully to restart the engine. He fiddled around and the engine coughed, started and proceeded to run smoothly.

"The selector switch was set on an empty tank."

Red-faced, I realized I had been up flying long enough to run the left wing gas tank dry. I hadn't remembered to switch to the half-full right one.

After a strong reprimand, I was allowed to continue flight training. The occasion did have a positive ring though; I never again landed on an empty tank. On an even more positive note, I felt a new flying confidence emerging from the manner in which I'd managed the emergency landing situation.

A Gotcha Scam—Luke Army Airfield—July 1942

By the tail end of July 1942, most of us successful basic training boys were ordered transferred to Luke Army Airfield, Arizona. This was an advanced flying school, about 30 miles northwest of Phoenix. I succeeded in gaining special permission to travel by car with a buddy, Hank Schneider. I think he was the only cadet in the class who had a car with him. The rest of our class went by train.

Hank was particularly proud of his car, a 1934 Ford convertible. It was one of the first of the Ford V8s, and was in immaculate condition. The 115-degree July sun torched through the glass, canvas and metal of that little coupe. There was no air-conditioning in those days but to make this ordeal trivial, bang went a rod and we coasted to the shoulder of the road with a dead engine! Interstate Route 10 to Phoenix was hardly traveled through the desert at that

Close-call Landing with a Dead Engine Award
Photo courtesy of Bob McCampbell

time. Luckily, before critically dehydrating, we were picked up and dropped off at the nearest sign of civilization. This was a last chance gas station and general store resting a good 50 miles from anything, any direction.

The store owner had a tow truck and recovered the coupe. To condense an ensuing, painful episode of bargaining, Hank was forced to sell his pride and joy for $50. Cars weren't being produced during the war and cars like Hank's were invaluable. Facts were, we had to be at Luke by role-call at 5 a.m. or we would be washed out of flight training for being AWOL ... even for an hour's shortfall. This great patriot of last chance desert enterprise knew he had Hank in a bind.

Heat Prostration Protest

So swearing to get even some day, we hitchhiked toward Luke into the wee hours of the morning. We arrived for about an hour of sleep and then a rude awakening at 5 a.m. Following a dawn patrol of drilling and calisthenics, we were allowed a quick breakfast and were back out on the concrete grinder. There in the blistering sun we stood at attention while being welcomed by the commandant. Mind you, we were in heavy wool, winter cadet uniforms including jackets and ties. The desert temp was beginning to reach for its daytime average of 115 degrees F. We were dripping wet and a couple of people passed out while we listened to a sermon on how our new leader was going to make men out of us, or else.

We then endured about an hour more of tough calisthenics. This torture included pushups that actually blistered my hands on the concrete surface. I could hear moans and murmurs of threats to "kill the SOB Commandant." This was only the beginning of the fulfillment of the SOB's promise. The pressures of an expedited flight training program would have been enough. But this was in a surreal setting of stifling round-the-clock heat compounded by lousy living conditions and relentless efforts by the command to make cadet life miserable 24 hours a day.

Cal Aero had been strict but meals and quarters had been excellent. Luke, in contrast, served barely palatable meals with diarrhea as a common companion. We lived in crowded open barracks with two-tiered bunks. The spaces did have evaporative coolers and the nights were almost tolerable when the coolers worked. Gang showers and a row of open toilets rounded out the creature comforts.

Desert Despair

There were no real recreational facilities, no off base passes, no girls at whom to make passes. We jogged daily in the midday sun for a little over a mile to a treeless, arid, physical training site. It wasn't unusual for one or more of our flight of about 30 cadets to pass out and fall along the way. When we arrived at the sports site we did a half-hour of uninterrupted, thermal-baked calisthenics. We then staggered onto a dusty desert baseball field or volleyball court with no real energy or interest left for such otherwise desirable sports.

The flight instructors (all army officers) even abused the sanctity of the flight line by conducting some more calisthenics before taking to the sky. One thing that certainly helped me all through the physical rigors of cadet days was my youth. I was 18 and 19 during my cadet training while a good number of colleagues were six or seven years out of school and out of shape. Naturally, the physical stuff had some merit, but it was the added burden of boredom, discomfort dysentery and gotcha rules that made life in the sand and cactus beastly.

Air Escape

The one escape from all of this was the flying. The North American AT–6, our advanced trainer, was a gem as were all North American products. The AT–6 was a low wing, 2-seat, 600HP radial engine aircraft with retractable landing gear. It had one 30–caliber machine gun in the wing and a small bomb rack. It was easy to learn to fly and pretty good on aerobatics considering its rather heavy, rugged construction. We had only military instructors at Luke and they were predominately excellent.

So, in spite of the expeditious nature of the flight training and each cadet's scramble to keep up, flying the AT–6 was much more rewarding and relaxing than the ground duties at Luke. Up a few thousand feet off the desert floor it was cool in more ways than one. On the ground

Advanced Trainer - North American AT - 6
Photo courtesy of Richard Bibb

you felt lower than the lowest private and you really were, in terms of treatment. In the air and in control of an airplane of a power and sophistication that even our recent Cal Aero instructors would probably never experience, you felt you had exceeded your wildest dreams. We flew formation as well as many hours alone doing aerobatics and other assignments. We flew night navigational trips and practiced some air to ground gunnery but unfortunately no aerial gunnery.

Grateful Glow and Gridlock

I dreaded night formation flying. I didn't realize it at the time but I don't think I ever could see well at night. I clearly remember gluing my eyes on the next plane's exhaust stacks, which brightly but narrowly illuminated my void and gave me a modicum of depth perception. A nervous night was had by all during touch-and-go landing sessions at an auxiliary base nearby. About 50 airplanes participated at one time with half of them circling, landing and taking off to the left of the runway and the other 25 to the right.

The airstrip was a wide four-lane rectangle allowing as many as four planes approaching, four more touching down while another four taking off. Moving airplanes surrounded me in the limited air and runway space like a bug-infested summer evening. Just one mistake in this melee could well wind up like autos piling on endlessly in a foggy freeway smashup. Somehow, we got through this phase with no major accidents. A few other classes were not so lucky.

Metamorphosis

I wondered from the beginning if I were destined to be one of those really hot fighter pilots. I was not one to take what I considered clearly unnecessary risks ... which some of my cohorts were beginning to do. On the other hand my confidence was growing in the basics such as aerobatics, formation flying, short runway landings and navigation. Generally good ratings on my check rides were confirming my skill and I was winding up flying the good ol' AT–6 with a smile.

A noteworthy event occurred at Luke in early September 1942, the final month of my cadet training. In recent months an increasing number of cadets had been washed out of training, apparently for trivial, non-flying rules violations. This was happening to senior cadets nearing completion of pilot training. Understandably, the commanding general of the Air Corps Training Command was simultaneously struggling to satisfy his boss by producing pilots faster than the enemy did. Could our beloved colonel, the commandant, be unwisely clogging the pipeline? Out of the blue, came an army of brass and inspectors, creeping through the cactus, asking questions. This investigation didn't last long. Neither did our beloved commandant, Colonel SOB Himmel. He was shipped out and replaced.

Life on the ground at Luke changed overnight, but most of the changes came too late for our class. We missed out on the swimming pools and new quarters, but meals and general treatment improved immediately. We even got time off in Phoenix.

The Finish Line

If it looked as if the Angel of Cadets ... and of mercy ... was winging her way to bless your graduation and commissioning, the first thing you had to do was get into town and finalize a uniform order.

I did just that and contributed to a local clothier's first million. My buddy Jimmy McCauley and I had obtained an overnight pass and rented an air-conditioned motel room with a refrigerator. We got measured and made down payments on our glory uniforms of pinks and greens. This was the WWII, U.S. Army Officer dress uniform, including steel gray trousers and a dark green jacket and cap. We then spent the time remaining reveling in the comforts of gourmet dining, cold beer and a good bed.

The great day, September 29, 1942, finally came. Of most symbolic significance to us at the time, was the award of the Silver Wings uniform adornment. Of really more importance, I received my orders commissioning me a 2nd lieutenant in the U.S. Army Reserve and placing me on active duty as a qualified military pilot. I use the term finally because it did seem an interminable series of physical and mental hurdles to overcome en route. On the other hand, to think that I metamorphosed from an 18-year-old stock boy into a

19-year-old officer and gentleman and military pilot in less than nine months, was mind-boggling.

Never again would I experience such an overnight change in my status, way of life and self-esteem. One day I was a lowly cadet with less clout than a raw recruit. The next, I was someone admired on the street, or even saluted ... a leader of men. My dad drove the 300 miles from Ventura to see me graduate. Although he never had been really critical of me, I'd given him little to brag about. Finally, at this moment, it was his chance to be proud. Mom was living in Santa Barbara and I visited her soon after graduation. I believe she was too frightened of the whole situation to attend a ceremony in its honor.

Officer and Gentleman
2ⁿᵈ Lieutenant Robert McCampbell
Photo courtesy of Bob McCampbell

Mom & Bob in Santa Barbara
Photo courtesty of Bob McCampbell

Chapter 4

Scary First Duties
Air and Ground

An Officer and a Gentleman—1942

My orders read, "Report for duty, to Commanding Officer, 79th Fighter Squadron, Army Air Base, Paine Field, Everett, Washington." This is where the huge Boeing plant is today. My orders allowed me a few days delay in route for a home leave in Santa Barbara. It was heartwarming to see my parents, old friends and of course, my high school girlfriend, Jo McCarthy.

The adulation I received from my uniform was almost embarrassing. Privately, I enjoyed the attention, but peripherally I questioned whether I could live up to everyone's expectations. I'm sure most of my colleagues also wondered how we would fare in combat. The war had not gone well thus far. Looking back, even our nation's leaders had serious concerns about the eventual outcome.

At home and in every city and town the unified spirit of the people was apparent in every walk of life. Kids collected scrap metal; moms donated pots and pans and helped in canteens for servicemen, while men not in uniform volunteered as air raid wardens. But most significant, young women went to work *en mass*, manning jobs in the defense industry, earning the nickname Rosie the Riveter. In the workplace and in relationships, the male-female juxtaposition would never be the same. But nineteen-year-old 2nd lieutenants didn't realize that at the time.

First Flying Duty

The Army flew me via commercial DC–3 to Seattle and then a train to Everett, Washington. I remember passing the Boeing plant (then only in Seattle) and seeing a giant tail protruding from a hanger too small to house it. It turned out to be the B–29 Superfortress experimental model that almost two years later wreaked havoc on Japan.

I reported to my new squadron commanding officer at Paine Field and was happy to find my old flying school buddy, Jimmy McCauley, holding a bunk space in his assigned BOQ room (Bachelor Officers Quarters). Other friends from Luke were also there and had been whooping it up nightly in the Officers Club bar. I had been to a few bars during my training, but was not a big drinker and still under-age in most places, although servicemen were rarely challenged in commercial bars. But here protocol almost demanded attendance by officers. In fact, our CO regularly held squadron meetings there on Friday or Saturday nights and conducted sing-alongs of old favorites. I got along well since he appreciated my tenor harmony.

Airplanes are Rationed Too

To our dismay, we only had one tired P–39 Airacobra airplane per squadron. That still was exciting because we had seen movies extolling the virtues of the P–39 and couldn't wait to check out in a real fighter plane of such stature. Only two problems remained. First, there was rarely a plane available to fly. Everything was either being shipped to combat forces or our single plane was grounded for mechanical problems. Second was the lousy flying weather dominating the Pacific Northwest.

Finally Fly a Fighter

The day came when the major strapped me in the cramped cockpit and sent me off to an even greater disappointment. Although we had spent some rainy days studying the characteristics of the P–39, it and all fighters of that era were single seat aircraft. There were no dual checkout rides with an instructor as there had been in flying school. It was flee-or-fly on the first flight. Even with such trepidation I was still anxious to feel the power and speed of this beauty.

The P–39 was a unique airplane. Its aerodynamic design rendered a sleek and aesthetically exciting profile. Its engine was uniquely placed directly behind the cockpit. A hollow drive shaft to the propeller ran under the pilot's seat and between his legs, protruding through the nose. Contained in the drive shaft was a 37 mm cannon that fired through the propeller hub. The nose compartment housed the cannon

P – 39 Airacobra
Photo courtesy of WarbirdAlley.com

rounds. The cockpit was covered by a fixed, reinforced Plexiglas canopy. A car-like door on each side served as the only cockpit access or exit. All other fighters of all nations were accessed via a sliding or hinged-opening Plexiglas canopy that was manually ejectable in an emergency. The P–39 also had tricycle landing gear, another novelty among single engine fighters.

I taxied this maverick to the runway, reluctantly pushed the throttle to the bottle (oxygen) and started pulling it off at about 130 mph. It reluctantly left *terra firma* and gradually climbed out over the ubiquitous pines. The rate of climb and the airspeed were disappointments. Moreover, the controls felt mushy, akin to power steering in an older car with too much play in the wheel. Things felt a little better as I gained altitude and airspeed. I felt the plane was flying me rather than the other way around and I was damned glad to get it back safely on the ground.

By autumn, we had received a few more planes and consequently, gained more confidence and flight time in the 39. However, mostly due to weather, I gained precious few flying hours and little proficiency as a fighter pilot in the months at Paine AAB. On the other hand, my social life improved and I had a ball. How could life be otherwise for a single, 19-year-old fighter pilot? We frequented the dance halls, especially the Swedish polka palaces, where we drank beer, whirled the girls, and later nursed hangovers. The local girls couldn't wait to be invited to the officers club, which got a little wild on Friday and Saturday nights. McCauley and I also enjoyed tromping through the back roads and trails. We crossed the many waterways on bridges and small ferries, and visited quaint villages in the Washington forests.

Protecting the Home Front at a Desk

I had an interesting temporary assignment in December 1942. I was sent for training at a filter center in Seattle. The center continually plotted the positions of area planes and ships via radar and visual sightings. It was a large oval room containing a massive table. Covering it was a giant sector map reminiscent of a movie on the Battle of Britain where such centers provided the information for air defense against the Luftwaffe. Several women soldiers (WAACS) wearing headphones and carrying cue stick-like poles, moved around the table repositioning little replicas of ships and planes. Skirting the table work area were offices of various duty officers, including one for a general in charge of everything should the shit hit the fan. Circling the plotting table on a level above were separate, glassed-in cubicles for various duty officers of lower rank (like me) with specific liaison responsibilities. Each cubicle had an instrument panel consisting of phones and an intercom with several colored buttons. This was to be my home away from home for a couple of nights.

Knowing little about what I was getting into, I reported for duty one winter evening and was sent up to the fighter control cubicle to relieve another 2nd lieutenant. He gave me a quick briefing on my duties and how to work the system, adding, "nothing ever happens in this boring place anyway." As the evening dragged on, I watched the WAACS add, subtract and reposition a few ships and an occasional aircraft on the plotting table. All, of course, had been friendlies.

I was fighting off a nap about 1:00 a.m. when people began to stir below. A few officers gathered around the plotting table and a frenzy of activity erupted. Suddenly, a red light flashed on my console. I answered my intercom and learned that a large un-identified flotilla had been spotted a couple hundred miles off shore in our sector. I was big time nervous! The ill-defended west coast of 1942 was of concern at all levels. Ever since Pearl Harbor, the country feared a coastal attack by Japanese naval and air forces and even a ground invasion.

When the general and other high-ranking army and naval officers appeared, things got hot, heavy and confusing. The WAACS feverishly tried to plot the possible enemy flotilla, whose size and location were based on scant information from a U.S. tanker heading west. I was to alert the CO of three fighter groups in the Washington/Oregon areas for each to ready his pilots and planes and to standby for further instructions. The COs were as confused as I was and asked endless questions, for which I had few answers.

My next cubicle counterpart, the bomber control officer, was equally confused. He had to get bombers armed and off to find the flotilla. I merely had to find an airborne enemy and direct our fighters to it. Simple. Except that it was mid-winter in the Pacific Northwest, dark, drizzling, with a zero ceiling and visibility. Radar systems were primitive. Not only was an intercept a poor bet , it was doubtful we'd recover many of our own aircraft if we launched in this weather.

In retrospect, the Japanese would have had worse problems returning to a carrier under those conditions. They'd been lucky to find the west coast. But at the time I could only imagine the possibility of being responsible for a worse military blunder than Pearl Harbor. Fortunately for me, (not to mention the country as a whole) the alert suddenly ended. Apparently, the tanker had spotted ships from our own fleet going somewhere unbeknownst to our filter center.

Runways are Too Short in the Northwest

As we prepared to move from Washington to a spot closer to my home, March Air Base near Riverside, a bit of flying misfortune befell me. With mixed emotions I had taken off in marginal weather for a short outing in a P–39. My emotions were more than mixed when I returned. The field was overcast and a light snow obscured the runway. After some wet palms flying around the area in and out of the soup, a small hole in the murk appeared next to the field. I dropped down to about 100 feet with the base in sight. With barely enough altitude to maneuver I made a tight turn and lined up with a runway. Oh Boy! I had too much speed and should have gone around, but visibility was too poor. I pushed the wheels of the tricycle gear onto the runway, pounding my feet on the brake pedals. I may as well have been pushing on a car clutch as I skidded on the wet snow, went off the end of the runway and nosed up in a ditch. I was going too slow to get hurt, but I bent the prop and drive shaft on the P–39. My CO also bent my fitness rating a bit downward.

A few days later I was assigned as control tower duty officer. On my watch, a P–38, twin engine Lightning fighter landed under similar, very low visibility conditions. As I had done, he came in too hot and I knew was heading for trouble before he touched down. We used radio and a cascade of red flares, urging him to go around for another approach to no avail. Over the end of the runway he went, bending two props and drive shafts. I wondered if his mistake was reflected double on his fitness rating.

Chapter 5

P – 39 Fails
Obedience Class

Dear Old Dad and a Duty Change – 1943

We had a wild New Year 1943 party in a downtown Everett hotel and soon thereafter began our move to March Field, near Riverside, California. I can't remember the exact numbers, but there were not nearly enough P–39s for each pilot to fly there. So some, like me, flew commercially and others were allowed to drive their own cars.

I stopped by home and picked up the '37 Plymouth coupe my Dad had given us in 1940. It was a great car for its time. By 1943, my Mom had arranged transportation through friends since gas was almost impossible for her to get. I wasn't exactly sure where I was going to find it either.

1937 Plymouth "War Machine"
Photo courtesy of Bob McCampbell

As the country moved into overdrive war production, shortages of almost everything began to arise. This necessarily led to implementation of a federal rationing system with a board and an office in every sizable community. Each adult was issued a monthly ration book containing coupons for shortage items, such as gas, tires, and meat and certain other food items. The ration coupons were tailored to your job needs and number of kids to feed.

That's a bare outline of a rather complicated program but you got very little gas ration unless it was deemed necessary for a defense job or to a business requirement. A fighter pilot got no sympathy at all from the system unless he happened to have a dad who ran an oil refinery.

So on the way south from Santa Barbara, I stopped by Ventura to see my Dad at his Seaside Oil Refinery. My Dad, of course, immediately saw that his patriotic duty was to assure that a defender of the country had enough gas to get to his base and defend it. Away I went with a feeling like finding the pot at the end of the rainbow. Gas was gold.

A Brief Tour of March Army Air Base

Southern California's freeways are infamous for their gridlock miseries and getting through Los Angeles, in the pre-freeway era, was a painfully slow process. There were traffic signals at each intersection in the downtown and larger suburban areas. Eventually I made it to Riverside, California with gas to spare.

March AFB was one of the few permanent air bases in the country, blossoming out of the early post WWI era. Instead of tar paper shacks and gravel roads, here were permanent buildings, hangers, paved streets and recreation facilities. Family residential areas and bachelor quarters, the officer's and enlisted clubs and many other permanent facilities were handsomely styled in Spanish architecture including red tiled roofs. This was all landscaped in nicely gardened lawns, trees and plants. I had read about and seen pictures of March in my airplane magazines. It gave me a thrill to think I was now a part of such a shrine.

We were at March for less than a month when I started making the trip home to Santa Barbara on weekends using a few ration coupons and patriarchal refinery donations. On one such weekend the squadron CO was to be away through Wednesday of the week so I decided to extend my trip through the same period. On a Monday eve in Santa Barbara, got a wire from my pal, McCauley, saying the CO had returned to March that day and was angry to find so few pilots around the flight line, and for me to get my tail back ASAP. I jumped in the car that night and with less than a half a tank of gas and headed south to my Dad's place in Ventura. As bad luck would have it my Dad was gone away on an overnight business trip.

I was able to reach him by phone and he suggested that I add a five-gallon can of cleaning naphtha to my tank from one he kept in his garage. He assured me the octane was adequate and that the naphtha, when added to the amount of gasoline I described as remaining in my tank, would get me to Riverside. I limped into the gate at March AFB in the wee hours of Tuesday morning with the gas gauge reading empty for the past 20 miles.

After a mild chewing out by the CO, I went back to my duties. These were mainly ground school and a few officer indoctrination efforts designed to orient me as an officer and something more than just a throttle jockey. We missed out on a lot of flying time because Southern California was having one of its wettest winters on record. We did get some unsolicited practice in landing in downpours.

Tonopah Turbulence—Bombing & Gunnery Range

Come the end of January we got orders to move the squadron to the bombing and gunnery range at Tonopah, Nevada. It was at this point I that made an unwise decision. I married the girl back home. This did not work out well for either of us in the post war years. So, with utmost respect for Lois, my dear wife and best buddy of now over 40 years, further references to this unfortunate wartime marriage will be sketchy. Suffice it to say Jo McCarthy and I eloped to Tonopah, a small mining town in the desert, midway between Las Vegas and Reno, Nevada. We were the ripe old age of 19 at the time.

Tonopah was about as forlorn and desolate a place as one could find in the west. It was high desert, and dropped down to zero degrees and snowed occasionally during our mid-winter stay there. Its chief claims to fame were gambling halls, a sporting house and a few shootings over a weekend. It was a virtual movie set for the wild west with miners coming in for Saturday night and buying drinks for the crowded bar. A favorite memory was the one-armed blackjack dealer who dealt cards faster than most two-handers.

The Army Air Forces base was not any dream spa either. Not that we needed any shade but trees were hard to find and family housing was not available. The base had been thrown together quickly in the high desert and was about as big a contrast to March Army Airfield as an outhouse was to the Waldorf Astoria. It did have some airplane hangers and a good long runway. It also had a bunch of bombing and gunnery targets scattered in the vast wastelands. Soon we were busy using these runways and targets daily.

Hate to say things about people and airplanes, but the P–39 Airacobra was no easy machine for dive-bombing, but if it was good for anything, it was great for strafing or air to ground gunnery. With the engine behind the cockpit the pilot was sitting well forward and for hedgehopping he could see the terrain better than in other single engine fighter. The armament arrangement was rather poor but fun for boys. It was a 37 mm cannon firing through the nose, two 50–caliber machine guns firing through the prop intervals and two 30–caliber machine guns in each wing.

The first problem was the relatively slow rate of fire for the cannon and its propensity to jam. Even without a jam, hitting a fast-moving airplane would be a real piece of luck with that Big Bertha. Then you had the four 30–caliber wing guns, which became obsolete by early WWII. Finally the two 50–caliber guns were too few. Their rate of fire was also slowed a bit by the synchroniza-

P – 39 Airacobra
Photo courtesy of USAF Museum

tion process, which enabled them to be fired safely through the propeller arc. In contrast the P–51 had six 50–caliber machine guns mounted in the wings and the P–47 had even eight. The wing mounting eliminated the need for prop-synchronized fire and therefore the rate of fire was faster.

I never felt very pleased with my dive bombing accuracy and most of my squadron guys shared this concern. One problem was we got relatively little practice. Another was the absence of dive flaps. Dive flaps allowed pilots of planes built strictly for dive-bombing to better hold the vertical position so necessary for accuracy in the dive run. I did feel good about my accuracy in strafing runs (air to ground machine gun targeting) and this activity was especially risky for the inexperienced. Two pilots were killed firing at ground targets while we were at Tonopah.

The deepest of several pitfalls in strafing was that while necessarily flying very low it was easy to get mesmerized by the target. To hit a target on the ground with the fixed guns of a fighter, the pilot obviously must aim the nose of the plane down. If you are already brushing the cactus when you do that, the cactus will be your resting place. I had some close calls on these runs. It might be worthy of mention, that ever since WWI, the conceptual aura of combat between opposing fighter planes has conjured up glamorous gladiator imagery and legends. In reality, the most risky business of the fighter pilot in World War II was combat against ground targets.

You may have noticed something missing thus far from our training experiences. I don't recall ever practicing any air-to-air gunnery while at Tonopah. *Would we never have need to fire at a flying enemy?* The only way to practice such skills at that time was to use a light bomber to tow a sleeve. This was a wind-sock or banner the size of a fighter fuselage at which a practicing fighter could make limited angles of attack and fire one of his fighter's weapons at the sock.

For obvious reasons the pilot was limited to fir-ing at angles that did not endanger the tow plane, an exercise far better than no aerial gunnery at all. I guess that the best training we found in this respect was our occasional practice dog-fighting amongst each other when the situation allowed. The object, always, was to get behind the other plane's tail. Needless to say, no weapons could be fired, so this equated somewhat to kid's cowboy-like I gotcha! practice.

Requiem for a Fearless Leader

Aside from the awful living conditions for the few married pilots who necessarily squallared it out in town, another pilot concern of more serious interest arose. We had acquired a new gung-ho CO reassigned from the early combat in the South Pacific. By this time we had lost three more pilots to P–39 accidents. Two of these involved spin-ins while practicing aero-batics. Needless to say, several of us were becoming openly apprehensive about the risky characteristics of the airplane in such necessary fighter tactics.

Well, what do you know? The new CO hardly gets his long-johns on (it was cold on the flight line) when he calls the squadron together for a separate-the-men-from-the-boys admonition. He says,

"I know some of you are running scared about the stall characteristics of the P–39. I'm here to tell you that you can do anything in that airplane that can be done in any fighter airplane. We're going to start some real flying around here and each man is going to wring out these little SOB P–39s till they say uncle! I want you each to follow my ass in everything I do in that airplane or turn in your wings and take over the mess hall."

Now, I was really worried. More and more horror stories were beginning to leak out about that plane. Still, we all had to acknowledge that our leader had come to us with some exceptional credentials. Not only was he one of the first pilots we had come across with aerial combat experience, but also he was the only one we'd ever see with a degree in aeronautical engineering. Finally, the new boss was not just a do-what-I-say leader. Right after his sermon, he spun rubber in his jeep to the flight line, jumped in his P–39, and shoved the throttle to the wall. He proceeded to conduct a breathtaking, one man, low altitude aerobatics show, right over the runway. No question, it was truly inspirational that anyone could safely perform such maneuvers in a P–39.

Yet, as the exemplary flying demonstration faded, I was left worried about his digging a deep flaming hole in that unfriendly desert. I guess I really was more worried about digging my own hole while trying to do the same stuff.

Now comes the sad, dramatic twist to this story. A few days later our inspirational CO was again performing some aerobatics in his P–39; this time at a higher, safer altitude. Appallingly, he encountered the infamous P–39 tumble and flat spin and dug his deep hole in the desert before I had a chance to dig mine. Aerobatics in the P–39 were restricted nation-wide, pending Air Corps-wide investigation. God rest a gutsy CO.

The P – 39 Gets Bad Press

Sometime in early 1943 a nationally syndicated news article featured an interview with a U.S. fight-er pilot newly stationed in England. This pilot was a member of an American P–39 Squadron, one of the first Army Air Corps units to be sent to England in WWII. The P–39 Squadron had not yet been assigned to a combat mission. The pilot had been selected to fly a Spitfire with an RAF squadron on a fighter sweep over the occupied continent.

As I recall, the sweep involved a chance engage-ment with enemy fighters. Hence, the U.S. press had anxiously awaited an interview with one of the first U.S. Air Corps pilots to experience combat in Europe. I can only paraphrase a few of the pilot's words to the press. They went something like, "God I'm sure glad I wasn't in a P–39 up there."

Congress demanded an explanation and Air Corps Chief Hap Arnold stepped on the carpet and tried to explain. Seems to me the explanation had something to do with the fact that our fighters, such as the P–39, were built for specific purposes and ... well ... seems fighting enemy airplanes wasn't one of them. I understood that the guy who crash-landed on Hap's carpet was the poor P–39 pilot who had been selected to fly a Spitfire by the RAF.

With all my criticism of the P–39 Airacobra, I must give the devil its due. It was an admirable de-sign concept what with its aerodynamic contours, its engine behind the pilot, the tricycle landing gear, its cannon through the nose and all. Also, in deference to its designers, the Army, admittedly, had insisted on some modifications that proved detrimental to its performance.

Still, it doesn't take an aeronautical engineer to raise an eyebrow at the center-of-gravity risks inherent in a fighter with an engine stuck behind the cockpit, counterbalanced by heavy, expendable cannon rounds in the nose. Secondly, it's tough to excuse the builder, Bell Aircraft, which promoted the P–39 with a campaign of hype far exceeding its capabilities and actual accomplishments. Many young, inexperienced pilots, including three close friends, were killed while training in the P–39. Bell and the Army should have been much more aggressive in pilot warnings and remedial advice covering the P–39's dangerously unique stall characteristics. Mercifully, superior, safer U.S. fighters soon supplanted the vaunted Airacobra.

Santa Rosa and the Russian River

February 1943, our squadron was transferred to Santa Rosa, California, a beautiful little rural town about 40 miles north of San Francisco. A bunch of us newly married settled down into cabins along the nearby idyllic, forest-framed, Russian River. It probably was a five or six country mile commute to our Santa Rosa Army Air Base. My stay there was covered in a December 5, 1993 column published in the Santa Rosa Press Democrat. It had been on the advent of the base's 50th Anniversary that a columnist requested my recollections. I'll summarize my published input reflecting Santa Rosa's blessings and our tragedies.

First, what an incomparable upgrade in creature comforts and scenic surroundings greeted us in Santa Rosa! Occasionally we were reminded that our real purpose here was as a vital link in the San Francisco wartime defense perimeter. Otherwise, we might well have succumbed to the siren call to decadence. We roamed the countryside on bikes and in jalopies, both of which we also used for commuting to the base. We mingled in the San Francisco nightlife on a few outings and frequented the Saturday night dances at the nearby riverside town of Guerneville. Several of us found an exciting sport on the river. We'd haul a couple of kayaks up stream on a jalopy and ride the rapids back to our cabins. A group of us had planned a weekend ride to the river's Pacific mouth but the war got in the way.

We were in Santa Rosa to fly, train and by so doing, protect San Francisco. And fly we did. Among other things, we finally got in a few aerial gunnery hops, firing at a tow target pulled by a B–26 medium bomber. I could have used many more tries. For me, hitting the sleeve, using only one of the P–39's 30 caliber machine guns was comparable to duck hunting with a 22–caliber rifle instead of a shotgun. To make it really analogous, the hunter would have to be jogging toward the flying duck while firing.

We flew a few practice interception missions and some false alarm alerts where something always seemed to go wrong with the radar intercept process. While at Santa Rosa, I don't recall any successful radar-controlled interceptions. Luckily for our country, the Japanese never launched a serious attack on the continental U.S. Occasionally, a few of us could sneak off from a prescribed training situation for a favorite pastime; darting down to the bay area in our P–39's and picking an aerial dogfight with the indigenous Navy pilots. We always claimed we won each skirmish and I'm sure the Navy returned to their Treasure Island Air Station proclaiming the same. A rite of passage was flying under the Golden Gate Bridge ... and for those of sterner stuff, under the Bay Bridge. I sucked it all in when I one day yielded to peer pressure and scooted under the much lower Bay Bridge. Flying under either was punishable by court martial. We officers and gentlemen were post pubertal ... but not by much!

Gassed in the War

I might mention that, added to the inherent perks of life on the Russian River, was the availability of gasoline in a ration-tight world. We pilots called it moonlight requisitioning. It consisted of the simple system of siphoning left-over aviation gas from airplane drop tanks. Such leftover gasoline was dumped by the Air Corps and the drop tanks, when remounted on the planes, were refueled with fresh uncontaminated gas. Since the aviation gas was rated at 130 octane we'd dilute each car fill-up with a quart of motor oil. My '37 Plymouth ran great on that stuff!

Golden Parachute

Included in my news editorial was mention of my abandonment of a P–39 while it was trying its best to show me who was boss. Turned out, it wasn't me and out I went, but not before other arrogant attempts by the maverick to deny me that option.

Certain maneuvers in the P–39 were officially banned from time to time. Typically, the restrictions were lifted after a short period with little fanfare and even less clarity. In retrospect, the buck was more or less passed back down the line with interpretations left to squadron leaders. So predictably, full responsibility really boomeranged onto the lap of each individual pilot. This way blame for accidents could more easily seek out and rest at the lowest level. Some policy-maker probably was promoted to general for coining the proverb, "If you can't stand the heat, get out of the airplane."

Accidents continued to plague P–39s in incidents where pilots were merely performing accepted, and necessary, fighter maneuvers. Needless to say, the problem did not pass unnoticed by any of us. Still, open discussion of the situation was rare. Most of us felt obligated to test the limits and build some confidence in flying the airplane as a fighter. I was feeling this obligation one early spring day alone at about 12,000 feet over Santa Rosa. With a deep breath, I did a few loops and then an over-the-top Immelman ... no problem ... and how refreshing it felt! Then I initiated a series of contiguous, slightly climbing slow rolls with some confidence ... I'd already done the tougher stuff.

On my back, in the third roll, the plane did it ... Holy God! ... Whaaaaaa the Hell! as I stalled and tumbled downward ass over teakettle, at least three times, coming out slightly nose-high, in a flat spin. Of course, in a split second, I knew what the hell. I tried all I could imagine to recover ... dropped full flaps, and then the wheels ... trying to change the center of gravity ... Come on Baby! Drop your frigging nose! Rudders and stick flailed around impotently. I gunned the engine wide open and tried again to get the nose down for a normal spin recovery. No dice! I was falling like a leaf ... relatively slowly, but fast enough to kill me. So when I perceived I was running out of the government's altitude and into mine I knew ... Gotta get out of this damned thing!

Now, other conventional fighters had sliding canopies that you could jettison under such circum-

Open door on P – 39 Airacobra
Photo courtesy of Bob McCampbell

stances. The P–39 had a fixed canopy with two car-like doors. The hinges of each door could be released by pulling two small peripheral pins. The plane was in a left spin, but being right handed my immediate reaction was to go out the right door, shoulder first ... Wrong!

The disorientation and centrifugal force of the spin made any movement an awkward challenge. I was able to pull the door pins and lean my shoulder heavily against the door ... and ... nothing happened! Next ... with all the force I could muster I lunged shoulder-first again ... off went the door, shielding me on the way out for a nanosecond. The right side of my face and ear brushed along the hot exhaust stacks behind the cockpit and my hard head nicked the right horizontal elevator. I was momentarily knocked unconscious and have no memory of pulling the parachute ripcord. Miraculously, I was awakened with a jar as the main chute popped open and I gazed up at its never-to-be-forgotten, angelic womb.

Of course, the plane hit well before I did, flat as a pancake ... at last only a compressed monument to the P–39's determined and insidious flat spin. Thank God, no one on the ground was injured and the only casualty, a planted field. The chute and I came down, luckily, between trees in an apple orchard. There were several cars lined up on a country road bordering the orchard. As I moved toward the road, the nearest car held two pretty girls in a convertible. One hopped out of the passenger side to help me into their apparently immaculate car. I was such a mess, bleeding from a head wound, I gallantly declined their kindness. I accepted the next offer, this one from an old guy who, fittingly, drove a very mature pickup truck. He took me for medical treatment to a nearby rural clinic. Its resident country doctor sewed my head and anguished over what was to become of such young men as me who breathed forced oxygen, sped through the skies at 400 miles per hour and jumped out in parachutes.

Over the weekend of my bailout, there were three other P–39 accidents in the bay area. All but mine were fatal. Forty years later, while passing through Santa Rosa, I obtained a front-page headline article from the Press Democrat morgue which covered the four accidents. Another treasure for my scrapbook.

About a fortnight following my accident, a Press Democrat headline reported the fatal crash of a squadron buddy. The circumstances of this incident mimicked mine. But, in this one, my friend was found draped over the trailing edge of his airplane's right wing. Tragically, he had exited the P–39 too late as it pancaked into the ground from a flat spin.

Ranch Home Nearly Struck
'CHUTE SAVES PILOT IN PLANE CRASH HERE
Wave of Army Air Accidents Reaches Four in Northbay Over Weekend; Three Killed

The Press Democrat, Santa Rosa, CA, March 23, 1943

"Wave of Army Air Accidents Reaches Four in Northbay Over Weekend: Three Killed"

"Scores of residents of the Sebastopol area were given a thrill yesterday when they saw a young air corps lieutenant "bail out" of his disabled fighter plane and parachuted safely to the ground as the ship spun earthward to crash in an apple orchard. The young flyer, **2nd Lt. Robert H. McCampbell**, stationed at the Santa Rosa Airdrome, suffered lacerations of the face when he was dragged against the cowling of his ship. He was picked up by ranchers who drove him to the hospital for emergency treatment. Witness who saw Lt. McCampbell bail out of his ship said the plane was high overhead when the motor sputtered..."

Chapter 6

Off to War in First Class

Into the Wild Blue Wonder—Boca Raton, Florida

In early May, 1943, as spring was blossoming into warm swimming weather on the Russian River I was suddenly faced with the reality of my newly chosen profession. McCauley and I and four other squadron pilots got orders to report to Boca Raton, Florida for movement to overseas duty as replacement pilots. The four were all close friends from flying school days. There was Norman "Grampa" Gross, an Iowa cement plant supervisor who had squeezed into cadet training at the upper age limit of twenty eight years. James "Roomy" Hudson was another elder, who by virtue his two years of college, had served as an elementary school principal in Arkansas. There was Ted "Abdul" Bullock whom, I believe, ran a dry cleaning business at home in National City, California. Indiana's Frank "Trib" Tribbett, another college student, rounded out our departing bunch. Among other things, we were all disappointed not to be remaining with the squadron, which was expected to be deployed, overseas soon with its current complement of officers and men.

With little fanfare, we loaded on to a DC-3 (C-47 Army Air designation) at about 3 a.m. one mid-May morn. Heading east out of San Francisco's Hamilton field were at least 10 pilots from other units joining us with the same orders. Can't remember how many stops we made chugging along toward Florida, but seems we touched down in West Palm Beach after sundown. I'll never forget stepping off into that warm breeze and those palms swaying into a personal greeting for us.

Vacation Won by Democratic Vote

We unanimously decided to take a short vacation in West Palm Beach. For three days we did the night clubs, saw the sights, some of the guys found new loves of their lives and I did some body surfing in the warm Atlantic waters.

One of the pilots introduced us to a young lady who invited us all to a party at her home. The home turned out to be a rather large well-decorated beach place along the very high rent West Palm Beach shore. No it didn't turn out to be one of those houses but it did turn into one wild party with a range and quantity of food, bar stock and girls like I'd never seen. The hostess was attractive and thirtyish (pretty old for most of us). She had some sort of story but I never really figured out where she came by the impressive mansion or the backing for her warm hospitality.

Back Under Military Jurisdiction

It escapes me how we found our way to Boca Raton. Also can't figure exactly how we escaped retaining the buttons on our tunics as punishment for our unauthorized vacation. Some ranking officer chewed our butts, but it came to naught. Not more than a day or two at Boca and three of us were driven to a Miami hotel. It was wholly taken over by the military. We were given food in the dining area and a vague briefing followed. It seemed we were to be shipped out soon, somehow, somewhere. We were also told not to leave the building or our assigned rooms after a certain hour. Further, we were to remain incommunicado, including phone calls home.

About midnight, I was awakened by a chaplain who appeared to be giving me my last rites. He asked if he might communicate, whatever I wished, to my loved ones back home. This sobering interlude did prompt some thoughts and introspections as to just what my interrelationship with God was or should be. I did acknowledge that I had cast a few urgent calls for help in his direction and I thanked him for the results thus far. Soon after this shallow bit of soul searching, I was rousted out and down into the lobby. Here, I was reunited with my original group from the flight out from California.

It was yet in the wee hours that we were all whisked off by bus to the Miami Airport. The whole episode seemed surreal or maybe more like a B movie about international intrigue. Come to think of it, international intrigue was exactly what it was. Anyhow, it sure felt good to get back with McCauley and the rest of the guys even though we still had no clue as to where we were going

What awaited us at the airport was a four engine Boeing 307 Stratoliner. None of us had seen one before. A grand total of ten had been built and were in the process of being delivered to major airlines for international travel when the war broke out. The

Boeing 307 Stratoliner
Photo courtesy of Jesse Davidson Archives

Stratoliner had employed many of the design features of the B-17 Flying Fortress bomber. But it had an aerodynamically smart appearance. It was the first commercial carrier to have cabin pressurization. It was a big aircraft compared to the DC-3. This particular model was configured to accommodate a row of compartments, or luxury cabins, along the starboard side and open seating along the port side. The original enclosing panels to the luxury cabins had been removed to allow for additional seating.

As we boarded at about 3 a.m. we were handed sealed orders, to be opened at a certain point en route. I got a window seat and we all settled down for a long flight to wherever. One of my most vivid memories on lift off was watching the lights of the Florida coast fade away in the distance. I wondered, of course, if that would be a last look at my country.

After a couple of hours we stopped in Puerto Rico for a brief stretch within sight of our plane. Then we were airborne again and following a lot of card games and whither are we going guessing games, we arrived over Georgetown, British Guiana. This airport had been hacked out of dense high jungle. Our pilot, an experienced Pan Am fellow, settled down to a good landing on the field and taxied up near the bar at the British "O" club. Most of us had a beer and some food and hit the sack.

The following day we were up and off early for a flight over the Amazon Delta, destination, Natal, Brazil. We were relatively low over the river and most vividly were formations of thousands of brilliant flamingos coloring the vast, unforgettable delta scene. It was here that we were allowed to open our orders. As we had guessed by this time and direction, we were going to North Africa. This route would allow bridging the South American and African coasts at their narrowest Atlantic reach between Natal and Dakar, Africa. One must understand that the aviation world was still nervous about flying over longer ocean routes.

Just Monkeying Around in Natal, Brazil

We were welcomed to a U.S. Army tent city at Natal where we spent several days awaiting a flight across to Dakar. The reason for the delay was that a German U–boat, a few evenings before, had surfaced just off shore at the Natal runway's end and shot down a converted B–24 transport as it was taking off for a trans-Atlantic run. So we weren't exactly in a rush to get going until that situation got fixed. The beach there was marvelous, but most exciting, I made two acquisitions in Natal.

First, Grampa Gross and I each bought a little spider monkey from a boy selling them near the base camp. They were cute little guys with the faces of mature men and about 12 inches tall. Mine sat on my shoulder when he wasn't showing off. When Gross' and mine got together wild things happened. They'd jump at each other from their leashes and swing back and forth clasping hands and put on a real monkey performance. Their crazy antics prompted me to name my monkey Flat-Spin. I felt I was beginning to actually communicate with Flat-Spin by the time we packed to leave.

The other buy I made was a pair of very comfortable red leather boots. I recall I paid about four dollars for them at some marketplace in town. They were like engineer boots and I had gone on to wear them casually and frequently as flying boots. They slipped on and off so easily that they made great slippers or town wear. I decided to wear them throughout the war. If I'd ever had to bail out those boots would have kicked off long before the chute opened.

Refrigerator Liberator

An Allied anti-sub corvette soon began cruising off the Brazilian shore for protection and so we were quickly loaded onto a B–24 Liberator and bound safely for Africa. Grandpa Gross and I each got aboard with a monkey and a Val-Pac (pilot's hang up suitcase). The B–24 had been converted to accommodate about 20 passengers in semi-comfortable seating. We

B – 24 Liberator
Photo courtesy of WarbirdAlley.com

leashed the monkeys to the top of the pile of luggage up over the bomb bays. This was to be an 8 to 10 hour flight across about 1800 miles of the Atlantic.

We should have known better but most of us boarded in khaki shirt and pants uniforms carrying our leather jackets. It was one of the most uncomfortable nights I ever endured. The wind whistled through that sieve of a fuselage like a norther. Everyone shivered for most of the flight, especially the poor monkeys. They hugged each other for the whole trip. It's a wonder any of us survived. As the pilot eventually let down into warmer air along the African coast, the sigh of relief was deafening. It had been an indescribable, interminable nightmare of cold and sleeplessness. In retrospect it seems unconscionable that no one in Natal, including the B–24 crew, had warned us about the need for proper clothing.

On to Humphrey—Dakar, Africa—1943

We spent a couple of days in Dakar living in open barracks. On the first day, Flat Spin pooped on a major's cot. Gross and I decided our monkeys would be better off if they remained near the African jungles rather than continuing the trip with us to North Africa. So, with sadness, we cro-magnon-offs gave the two descendents of our mutual ancestors to a couple of GIs stationed at Dakar. I did realize that their acquisition in the first place had amounted to a wee bit of leftover adolescence on my part (I had turned twenty by now). Anyhow, after more great body surfing at the nearby beaches, we piled on an awaiting Air Corps C–47 workhorse and headed north.

We flew over the monotonously desolate Sahara for hours. It occasionally revealed a small group of Arabs and camels hundreds of miles from anywhere, seemingly headed nowhere. I didn't even see an oasis. Finally, an area of marked contrast loomed ahead and we landed at Marrakech, Morocco, a verdant Mecca even for us infidels. Unfortunately, we didn't get to see much of the place since we merely gassed up the old bird and chugged on to Bogeyville, as I called it, or Casablanca of Humphrey Bogart fame

Parts of Casablanca were green and attractive with some well-maintained middle and upper class residential areas. Europeanization had made it a fairly modern city with decent shops and department stores. Of course, there was also the Casbah, the ancient and mysterious walled Arab part of the city. For American military the Casbah was off bounds or forbidden territory. French Morocco was the site of the first landings by U.S. forces in the European Theater of WWII.

You Must Remember This

From the spring of 1940, through mid-1942, with the exception of the Battle of Britain, the war had not gone well for the Allies. France, with much of its army and equipment never committed, had capitulated to the Germans in June 1940, while Japan's successes brought it to the shores of Australia and to the eastern frontiers of India. Sinking of Allied shipping was mounting alarmingly. The USSR, having borne the full brunt of the German onslaught, was exhausted and demanding Allied action. Finally, in June 1942, the British forces in Libya suffered a major defeat at the hands of German General Rommel, The Desert Fox, and were driven back to El Alamein, toward the Nile delta in Egypt.

The Americans and British feared a Russian collapse, but were unprepared to invade western Europe. The Brits, over U.S. objections, devised a plan to invade North Africa, control the Mediterranean, and eventually invade the soft underbelly of southern Europe.

The invasion of western North Africa became largely an American effort that finally got underway in early November 1942, backed by a huge Navy task force. The landings took place at Casablanca and Oran in Algeria and were mainly opposed by the Vichy French; or French Government under German occupation. Fortunately, just prior to the invasion, the British, led by General Montgomery, scored one of the most startling and brilliant victories of the war, defeating Rommel at El Alamein, in western Egypt. Had Rommel triumphed, conceivably he could have linked with the Japanese moving toward the west. As the Americans were landing, the British were beginning a

750-mile trek across Libya toward Tunisia against the retreating Germans.

The untried Americans had a tough time getting on the beaches, suffering with capsized landing craft and other glitches. They succeeded only because the French put up only token resistance and were equally confused. In defense of the Americans, they not only were green but also had spent more than a fortnight on troop ships crossing more than 3,000 miles of ocean. Then they were dumped into pitching landing craft while taking fire from shore. What a lousy Mediterranean cruise!

Navy F–4 Wildcat fighters from a carrier engaged in some dogfights with French fighters, mostly Curtis P–36s sold to the French by the U.S. in 1940. Both sides lost planes. The *Jean Bart*, a French battleship, had been steaming out of the Casablanca Harbor to thwart the invasion when a 16-inch shell from a U.S. battleship hit its forward turret. It happened to be one of many duds (shells that failed to explode) fired by the U.S. Navy in the invasion. This half-ton dud glanced off the forward turret, down through the heavy steel top deck, wandered aft through bulkheads, and finally took out the officers' mess. When I later went on board this anchored French ship for a look, the huge unexploded shell sat upright on display just outside what was left of the officers' mess.

The French, who had little heart for conflict with the Americans, capitulated a few days after the invasion. After much political infighting amongst themselves, they sided with the Allies against the Germans. Initially, the U.S. and Free French troops from the west, and the British from the east, rapidly closed in on Rommel's troops concentrated in Tunisia. The German's back was to the Mediterranean. But Rommel, a sage, cagey general, obtained some ground and air reinforcements. He then counterattacked in thrusts east, west, and south inflicting serious casualties on all surrounding Allied forces. The situation remained fluid with hard fighting for a month or so, but the Allies prevailed. The final successful offensives were underway in May 1943, when my small group arrived in Casablanca.

[Unknown], Labarge, McCauley, McCampbell and Bullock
Photo courtesy of Bob McCampbell

Never is Heard a Discouraging Word? ... Casablanca

McCauley and I were riding in the back of a two-and-half-ton truck from the airport to downtown Casablanca with two combat-experienced, B–26 (light bomber) pilots who were picking up additional planes for their unit at the front. One asked what we were going to be flying. I confidently offered, "We were trained in P–39s and I'm sure that's what we'll be driving here." The other guy smiled. "Are you going to be able to get out of that duty?" McCauley and I looked at one another. Then these guys related how one P–39 Group had been shot up badly on the ground by strafing enemy fighters and then nearly eliminated in a couple of air encounters with ME–109s. We weren't nearly as confident on the trip back to base.

Bear Sh __

If you follow the camel dung about twenty miles south of Casablanca, you would find the quaint, but smelly Arab berg of Barasheed. It's pronounced like it appears, but the pilots referred to it as "Bear Shit." A fighter training center had been set up here by an enterprising general who realized that not only were the U.S. ground troops green, but also the fighter pilots. Somehow he had collected a few P–39s, P–40s, P–38s, and British Spitfire Mk–Vs. He had also gathered a handful of pilots who had combat experience and made them instructors. How these tight commodity resources had been spared is a mystery, as is how our small group landed at this place.

We were immediately assigned to some old P–39s but we got relatively new tents and cots. The sand blew through the tents and flies penetrated just as easily. I got severe dysentery and lived on paregoric through most of my time at Barasheed. I did get in some P–39 time during June, but in mock dogfights there was always a Spitfire or a P–38 winding up on my tail. Still, no aerial gunnery practice.

Achtung Schpitfuer!

Toward the end of June, McCauley. Gross, Bullock and Tribbett were assigned to Spitfire training. Roomy Hudson and I were not. I was disappointed because I desperately wanted to fly something other than the P–39, especially after McCauley told me what a great plane the Spit was. McCauley suggested I go to the director of training and cry on this guy's shoulder about my loss of confidence in the P–39 and my desperate need for a transfer to Spits. I built a tearjerker plea centered on my bailout in the States and laid it on the major. I think he finally transferred me to Spits to get me out of his hair. Roomy Hudson seemed happy to stick with the P–39. But we all were sorry to see one of our original six being sorted away

Why were they training U.S. pilots to fly British Spitfires? We soon discovered that two U.S. fighter groups had been outfitted with Spits as a reverse lend-lease gesture on the part of the British. So many billions of dollars in aid had been given to England by the U.S. that it became politically wise to make things look a bit more reciprocal. We lucked out.

The Spitfire was a dream compared to the P–39. It wasn't that it was any faster or that the controls moved easier. It was simply the immediate grabbing the air feeling one got on takeoff compared to the mushy feel of the P–39. Better yet, aerobatics could be done with confidence, and we could turn inside the U.S. planes ... always an objective in a dogfight. It was a new world in the air for me, especially when I heard that the only U.S. fighter groups with more victories than losses in the African campaign flew Spitfires.

Another War Communique

By June 1943, the Allies had overrun all Axis resistance in North Africa and captured 250,000 German and Italian soldiers. By mid-July, Allied troops had crossed the Mediterranean and invaded southern Sicily. The victory in North Africa was owed, to a great extent, to U.S. air superiority, especially the close ground support it provided and the interdiction of Axis supply lines. On the other hand, American fighter pilots, for the most part, had not fared as well as hoped against enemy fighters. This was partly due to the growing obsolescence of the American P–39s and P–40s, and partly because the pilots lacked experience and training in aerial combat. Nonetheless, Allied bombers and fighters prevailed. They had been especially effective in pounding airfields and other enemy targets in and around Sicily since April of 1943.

War Zone Job Search— HQ, 12th Air Force—Tunis

It was just a couple of days following the Sicily invasion that McCauley, Tribbett, Gross, Bullock and I and I were poured onto a B-17, destination, Headquarters, 12th Air Force in Tunis. This was a no first class flight of about 1,300 miles taking about 6 hours. When we landed in Tunis neither our pilot nor anyone else around could tell us how to get to 12th AF HQ. The entire area was one of mass confusion. Lots of ground troops were around, many boarding DC-3s for Sicily. With an address finally obtained, we hitched an Army truck ride downtown to the supposed reporting location. Arriving, we found that the place housed new military occupants who could only advise us that 12th AF HQ had relocated somewhere in Sicily.

We hitched another ride back to the Tunis Airfield. On the way we saw acres of wrecked enemy tanks and other equipment. There were a bunch of GIs in an open area near the airfield who were racing all kinds of German and Italian motorized equipment around a dirt track and having a ball. We weren't! So, when we got back and found our B-17 pilot still around, we told him he needed to fly us over to Sicily. "Hell no!" the answer, "They're shooting at people over there." We shrugged, got in a chow line with some Army GIs and felt a little better.

After failing to find any better lodging, we lay mattress covers on an unused airplane parking ramp. We draped ourselves with mosquito netting and bedded down for not much sleep with a Val-Pac suitcase for a pillow. Awakening at dawn, we found that the mosquitoes hadn't been bothered much by the netting. We then sat around for a biting discussion over our next best move.

Can't Find a Job in this War!

It was unanimous; we decided to find a pilot who was willing to take us to Sicily. We found one finally, a C–47 lieutenant loading on a group of U.S. paratroopers. This pilot told us that after he brought these guys to an airstrip near their unit, he knew where there was a newly arrived Spitfire outfit and would take us there. This sounded ideal so we jumped aboard and headed out across the Med.

The Sicilian campaign was moving swiftly at this point since, characteristically, the Italian Army wasn't putting up much of a fight. The Germans were regrouping in a line across eastern Sicily, pretty much leaving the western two thirds of the large island up for grabs. The two Spitfire groups had moved in, the 31st to Argento, in the southwest and the 52nd to Palermo in the northwest.

It's Lovelier the 2nd Time Around?

The paratroopers were on their way to Sicily for the second time. It seems they had suffered from one of the serious blunders of the war. German JU–88s had attacked the U.S. Navy and British task force ships in the heat of the landings. Shortly thereafter, who had wandered overhead but the waves of invading U.S. paratroopers in their C–47 transports. One Navy gunner mistakenly fired from a ship and soon the entire task force opened up and managed to knock down 22 paratrooper laden C–47s. Fortunately many of the victims survived and were picked up in the water. Some of those were now our passenger mates.

Continuing with our less harrowing saga, our providential C–47 pilot landed deftly on a dirt strip near a small Sicilian village and off-loaded the paratroopers. Then, as promised, our pilot flew us up the 40 or so miles to Agrigento. We could see the Spits parked around the airfield as we circled it.

One of the local ground crew steered us to the squadron CO's quarters, a small masonry building in a tent city. This was one of the three squadrons of the 31st Group. The other two were at small strips nearby. We asked the CO if he needed four trained pilots. He answered, "Damn it, I was begging for pilots in Africa, just got some Eagle Squadron transfers and I can't use any more at the moment. Why don't you guys try the 52nd Group up at Palermo? They might need some pilots."

We turned in unison to the C–47 pilot. "Well" he says, "I flew into Palermo yesterday. It's short runway with trees on one end and a big brick wall on the other. But, guess I could do it again." McCauley questioned how they got Spitfires in and out. The C–47 guy replied, "That's gonna be you guy's problem." So, off we went again still trying to land a job in the war.

The Palermo runway was an attention getter; especially with somebody else was doing the landing. A C–47 in capable hands, however, could be squeezed in and out of pretty tight places. This one was in such hands, thankfully, and as the guy caressed the tree-tops with the lowered landing gear just before touching down, he squeezed the Gooney Bird into the tight space with a little room to spare.

Palermo Air Base was an interesting tour destination. It had been an Italian military flying facility with well-built permanent buildings and a paved runway. There were a few wrecked German and Italian fighters scattered around and a squadron of Spits parked here and there in protective revetments. Some of the hangers and other facilities were a bit battle-scarred from Allied bomber raids. As we would later discover, the coastal city of Palermo itself was just another magic Mediterranean cosmopolitan mixture of antiquity and modernity.

Chapter 7

Bombed in Bar
and Barracks

Hired! Palermo Sicily—July 1943

The 4th Fighter Squadron CO, Captain Tim "Sam" Houston, was not happy about being awakened. Tribbett led the introductions including a word on our unemployment status. Houston sleepily responded,

> "Yeah, I can use you. Do any of you guys know how to fix a generator?" Tribbett agreed to try. Then the Captain further asked, "Any of you guys got any combat time?" We shook our heads "no."

Houston looked disappointed but gave us an obligatory briefing and told us where to find a cot in the two-story building next door.

The 52nd Fighter Group commanded two squadrons in addition to the 4th. Just across the runway was our 2nd Squadron. The 5th Squadron was stationed on an airstrip about 20 miles to the south. All three were equipped with British Spitfire Mark Vb fighter aircraft. This was much the same fighter as the earlier 1940 Battle of Britain model. The only major change was that four of its original eight, small caliber (303) machine guns were replaced with two twenty millimeter cannon on the Mark Vb wings. Two Mark 9 Spitfires, were also furnished to each squadron. These were reserved for alert standby duty, had significantly higher performance capability than the Mark Vb and were used to run down enemy photo reconnaissance intruders.

The squadron where we'd earlier been turned down for a job in Southern Italy was part of the 31st Group, the only other American Spitfire Group. While the squadrons of the 31st Group saw some action supporting the troops pushing the Germans out of Sicily

Bob & Supermarine Spitfire MK IX
Photo courtesy of Bob McCampbell

and in the fall covering the invasion of Italy at Solerno, it is impossible for me to understand why our 52nd group was tasked to do so little. In August, I flew 16 convoy patrol sorties escorting Allied shipping and some combat formation training flights. I learned a lot from the guys who had joined the 4th as transfers from the RAF to the U.S. Army Air Corps. But the convoy patrols were boring.

War Going On, You Know

One aspect of life that wasn't boring was the occasional night raid on Palermo. The Germans were gutsy, making low-level runs at night, mainly targeting the U.S. supply and escort ships in the harbor. They used JU–88s, the very versatile, fast, light, Luftwaffe twin-engine bombers. Nothing we could do about it at night. We had no lights on the airfield and no searchlights nor radar systems to locate the airborne enemy planes at night. Moreover, the JU–88s were as fast or faster than our now obsolete Spitfire Mark Vs. The JU–88s dropped flares on the harbor and near us which illuminated their targets but not themselves. During the German blitz, the RAF could do little to stop the Luftwaffe night-bombers from devastating London.

The Germans, then British, and finally the Americans, developed specialized night fighter planes and sophisticated integrated night fighter radar systems.

During the first German raid on Palermo we ran up on the two-story roof of our quarters to watch the late show. Our airfield and quarters were high enough on a hillside to provide an excellent panoramic view of the German bomb bursts on the city below.

One night following an afternoon performance for the troops by Bob Hope and his troupe, we watched as the enemy raiders hit downtown near Hope's hotel. On another occasion, we watched as they hit an Allied freighter and more spectacularly we saw one of the bombers crash, bombs and all, into General Patton's headquarters building. Patton had commandeered a large, lone, conspicuous structure perched on a hillside with a spectacular view of the city. It appeared accidental and not a

Captured JU – 88
Photo courtesy of Bob McCampbell

likely German deed, since they were skilled enough at warfare without resorting to suicide tactics. Patton wasn't there but it's likely that a few of his soldiers may have wished he had been.

On another night, after getting to such loge-seat raids, an American anti-aircraft battery located less than 100 yards away abruptly awakened us with ear-splitting fire. We flew down the stairs and out into the nearest slit trench. Two 500 lb. bombs hit close enough to feel some concussion, one demolishing a church across the street. That was the closest we had come to a real war. After that, McCauley and I left our loge reservations for others of sterner stuff. Again one might wonder why we didn't take off after these intruders, but our aircraft were not equipped in any way for night fighting. Without a lighted runway we probably would have suffered unacceptable losses just trying to get our planes safely back.

College Frat Days Revisited

In spite of the war I enjoyed my time in Palermo. A couple of the ex-RAF guys decided that each pilot should have an auto at his disposal, so they ventured

into the city with sidearms and official paper work, then commandeered an assortment of fifteen cars, taxis, and official city or state vehicles. They worked most of the day bringing them back. I asked if we might be depriving some poor Italian of his livelihood, but Smitty, a former Harvard dropout said, "Nawh, the only Italians that own cars are Fascists, so we've just liberated the cars from those bastards!"

Bob & "liberated" Italian taxi
Photo courtesy of Bob McCampbell

Patton Leather

A few days later McCauley and I were strolling down the main drag in Palermo when we saw a military motorcade with a three-star general flag flying from a lead staff car. Military motorcycle escorts surrounded it. We figured only the famed, idiosyncratic General Patton could be inside. As we moved out to the curb to watch the parade, the motorcade abruptly stopped. A full colonel stepped out of the general's car and spoke a couple of words through the rear window to Patton. The colonel, accompanied by a sergeant, saluted the general, made a snappy about face, and walked briskly toward us. The colonel faced us and stepped onto the curb so he wouldn't be shorter than we. We saluted and the colonel reciprocated.

"Lieutenants," he said sternly, "You are out of uniform. I need your names and unit designations." Apparently, our leather flight jackets constituted flying gear and were not to be worn off base. This was, of course, ridiculous in a war zone. We really had no uniform jacket other than the dress uniform jacket. I'd not even brought one of those over-seas. Ground troops had their field jackets and Patton had designed his own jacket. But that was Patton. A week later our CO called us in.

"How in the hell did you guys manage to find Patton to screw up in front of?" he began. "You can write my reply covering your company punishment and my admonition to the squadron to dress properly in town." He then dismissed us and went off muttering "Jeeze Christ, leather jackets."

Shoot-Out at Club Med

Everywhere the squadron went the first thing the pilots did was to construct and stock the bar. But this solemn task had already been done when we arrived in Palermo. The bar in this case had been provided by the building's former occupants, the Italian Air Force, or Regia Aeronautica. Their left-over wines and spirits had been Colt 45 pistol targets for our pilots who had arrived earlier. They advised that the target practice had been mandatory since, "the booze could have been tainted". Everyone had to be on the alert for available bottled beverages on any trip into town. The bar thus remained acceptably stocked.

Late one evening I was awakened by gun shots. Several of us simultaneously arrived at the bar to find two of the pilots loaded and playing rummy by candlelight. They had shot Mussolini's picture off of one wall and King Victor Emanuel off another. Both were laughing hysterically amidst their tallow-tainted paper currency. They sobered up fast when the CO arrived, angry at being disturbed.

International Harmony

The bar was our cultural center of sorts. Naturally, all topics of conversation began and ended with women. The most memorable bar times for me, though, were those of camaraderie in song. I had been raised in an atmosphere in which family and friends frequently gathered around my mother's piano and reveled in group singing. Attached to our squadron, intermittently, were British, Aussie, New Zealander, South Afrikaner and Canadian pilots. The Commonwealth chaps seemed more tightly bonded by singing their ballads in common than we Yanks. But learning their songs and joining in with a couple of other Yanks was a delightful experience for most.

Many of the lyrics were understandably ribald and irreverent. They were thematic of military injustices, screw-ups or buffoonery. Most were extremely clever and were parodies on borrowed, easy to sing, familiar tunes. After sixty years I still remember many of them. One unforgettable British song began spontaneously with someone singing a well-known limerick. Others eagerly joined in, especially for the chorus. As the chorus ended, the original soloist would call out and point to some poor soul at the bar to produce the next limerick. The process was repeated until some one failed to come up with one and was summarily run out of the bar. I learned a lot of limericks fast.

Limerick	Chorus
A lord's wife named Lady Jane Knoll	That was a very fine rhyme
Had an idea exceedingly droll	Sing us another one
At a masquerade ball	Much like the other one
Dressed in nothing at all	Sing us another one do
She backed in as a parkerhouse roll	

Heir Left No Air

The bar lived up to its reputation as a menace, with a few of the pilots hitting the sauce a mite heavy. The bar served me a lesson one morning after a night at the watering hole with my friend Ennis. Here was an only son and heir to a New England estate worth more than I could imagine. He had been nurtured in third-generation wealth and propriety. He was an incomparable sailor, a decent tennis player and one who regaled us with stories about his decadent youth. By his own admission he had been drinking a bit since the ripe old age of age of twelve.

On one occasion McCauley and I caught a bird and caged it within Ennis' mosquito net while he was nursing a hangover. As we hoped, Ennis became convinced that he had suffered from the DTs. But our cure backfired. Early the next morning, a hungover Ennis woke me and begged that I take his duty as the alert pilot on the flight line. Although not in the best of shape, I reluctantly agreed because nothing ever happened while on alert. Where had I heard that before?

So, I toted my sleeping bag down under the wing of the designated alert plane, sucked in some pure oxygen in the cockpit (pilot's sure cure for a hangover) then went back to sleep.

For alert purposes, we had two Mark 9 Spitfires, which had more powerful engines than our regular duty Mark V's. These Nines out performed their Battle of Britain predecessors and were used by our squadrons to chase the Germans' fast, stripped-down

McCampbell's Supermarine Spitfire Mk IX
Photo courtesy of Bob McCampbell

photo reconnaissance planes. The souped-up Merlin Rolls Royce engines gave the Spitfire a much faster climb rate and higher speed especially at higher altitudes. The engines were later adopted for the American P–51 Mustangs and manufactured in the U.S. by Packard Motor Company.

During the three months since my arrival at Palermo, the squadron had launched only six scrambles or actual takeoffs after unknown intruders. Given the low threat, I snoozed comfortably under the protective wing of this piston-driven mother hen. Each pilot pulled about six hours of duty each week, awaiting the radar blip of an unidentified plane moving toward our sector. The radar station was located on a nearby hilltop and had a phone line to our small control tower.

My sleep was disturbed every ten minutes by the crew chief warming up the Mk–9 engine. The plane was plugged into a large generator cart that saved the charge on the plane's internal battery. Suddenly, I heard the sounds of distant shots, rose up out of my bedroll, and saw red flares followed by green ones flying out of the control tower. Simultaneously, Smitty, my lead plane pilot, started his engine and yelled, "Lets go Mac!"

The adrenaline surged and I jumped in my Spit. I flicked the two mag switches, hit the starter buttons, and began to follow Smitty, who was already going for broke taxiing out. As I started to move, my crew chief waved madly for me to stop. The generator cart was still plugged into the plane! I stopped before causing any damage, and the poor panicked crew chief unplugged the generator cart. My first flight in an Mk–9 had got off to ignominious beginning. By the time I reached the start of the runway, Smitty was already off and climbing wide open. I wrapped the throttle around the firewall and got off. Holding the Mk–9 straight down the runway with the heavy torque of its powerful engine (pull of the airplane sideways in the direction of the turning propeller) was a challenge, but the rapid rate of climb was a thrill. I finally caught Smitty at about 20,000 feet

We eventually got a good fix by the radar guy and spotted a twin engine in the distance. We armed our guns and began to close. My God! My adrenaline was pumping! Seconds later, surprisingly, Smitty tightly turned away advising that the target was a friendly British Mosquito (light bomber) with a malfunctioning IFF. "Let's go home, Mac," said Smitty, as he rolled over into a split S and dove straight down with me trying desperately to stay with him.

Suddenly, I heard a loud crack, followed by a sudden explosive smack of freezing wind. My canopy had blown off and ... *Jesus! Is the whole friggin airplane coming undone?* So I reduced speed and called Smitty, who advised me to do exactly that. Felt better as I we leveled out and neither Smitty nor I could see anything else obviously wrong with my airplane. Still, I made a rather studied landing approach to our short runway. I was always fairly confident that I could do a three-point touch down in any Spit within the first one hundred feet of a runway.

The flaps and brakes of a Spitfire were operated by a compressed air system. When the flap lever is flipped, the flaps immediately drop to a 90-degree angle. Since there was no intermediary setting it was crucial that the pilot not be going too fast when he flips it, lest he wants to leave the flaps behind. It normally felt like a skyhook had reached out and suddenly grabbed the plane.

As I flipped the lever I thought, *how smooth these flaps are in the Mk-9.* To my surprise, I found myself sailing beyond a safe touch down spot. I gunned the engine and pulled up just in time to try again. By this time I realized that I had no operable flaps. So, I tried landing a second time at the lowest safe speed above a stall. Without flaps I tried dropping it short and brushed the treetops coming in. I sailed long, but thought I should make it with strong braking ... and it hit me as I touched down. *Strong braking? Christ! The air system's out! No flaps, No brakes!*

Typically, a landed airplane steers by rudder, somewhat as it does in the air. But, as it slows, the rudder becomes ineffective. At that point the plane must be steered by alternately applying right or left brake. The Mk-9 had almost finished its landing roll as it neared the stonewall at the end of the runway. It was also veering uncontrollably toward a C-47 parked next to the wall on my right. A ground crew scattered. With no compressed air to activate the brakes the Spit didn't tire of rolling without a fight.

I had one option. I pushed the throttle wide-open, kicked ultimate left rudder, and the thing spun around on one wheel. This allowed me to narrowly miss the C-47 and the wall, but the left wing tip grazed the runway. Also, the plane climbed up an unoccupied dirt mound and I found myself temporarily stuck trying to jockey the thing off by gunning the engine. The CO gave me a bad time about messing up the wing of his pet plane and the crew chief was a little upset. They were both lucky I hadn't totaled the plane.

International Tennis

The Italians left us more than just the bar. At the flight line back of the control tower were the remains of a red clay tennis court. I hadn't hit a tennis ball in about two years nor really had I thought about it. But one day the tennis bug bit. Fortunately, and unbeknownst to me, Captain Lee Trowbridge, the Operations Officer and Deputy CO, harbored the same notion as he passed by the court each day. Later, I learned that he had played on a college team somewhere in the east.

Somehow, Trowbridge and I discovered our mutual interest. We worked hard for a month with help from some Army equipment operators and got a playable tennis court together. We found some decent wood rackets and hermetically sealed balls in Palermo, and began playing every day. Since we found ourselves quite well matched we felt we'd stumbled onto a promised land in the middle of a war zone. For the most part, the other pilots and enlisted men had never seen any decent tennis and watched us with wonder. Several who'd played little or none began playing regularly as an occasional substitute for hitting the bars and chasing the local girls.

The fun only lasted a couple of weeks. I contracted malaria, then yellow jaundice, and spent most of November 1943 in bed. In fact, a young GI in my ward died from the jaundice epidemic. Major symptoms are a yellow body and an absolute aversion to food. After the war I met a former medical officer who had served in the zone when they had discovered that contaminated serum was the villain. On one occasion, some buddies brought me a bottle of hard punch they had concocted and soon thereafter I began healing. This sort of medicine was the last thing the medics would have prescribed on my recovery diet. But it worked!

A Pilot's Pilot

Meanwhile, the 4th Squadron had acquired a new flight officer sometime in October 1943. His name was Bob Hoover, and he was the best pilot I ever saw perform. I can comfortably make that sweeping statement now after reading a recently published accolade by General Jimmy Doolittle who said that "Hoover was the greatest stick and rudder man I've ever seen"

During the early days of the war some of the graduating pilots were rated as staff sergeants, (rather than 2nd Lieutenants) then later promoted to flight officers, a warrant officer rank. Bob was one such officer. By the time he joined the squadron he was well known, in pilot circles, as an aerobatics pilot. After the war he became a legendary test pilot and famous international aerobatics showman.

Hoover had gained experience testing aircraft when planes were shipped in from the U.S. and uncrated in Casablanca for assembly and testing. He loved to fly so much that he flew every airplane in the existing Air Corps inventory and logged as many hours as possible. He was a world-class pilot with great natural ability and skills, steel nerves, and who practiced endlessly. He put on shows for generals, admirals, and foreign dignitaries, and humbled other nations' pilots in aerobatics contests.

My favorite of his maneuvers occurred on my watch. Four of us, including Hoover, were sent from Palermo to Setif, in North Africa, to pick up additional Spitfires from the British air depot there. A C–47 flew us down to Bone, Algiers. We thumbed rides on French, British and Algerian military trucks and jeeps, traveling inland through the ancient city of Constantine to the nearby depot in Setif. It was a real kidney crusher and dirt bath that took most of the day. I had been assigned as flight leader and as such was in charge of the trip. We got our Spits from the Brits late in the day and I decided we'd fly to Tunis to spend the night. I didn't want to try to find our unlighted landing strip in Palermo at night.

In the early morning we boarded our steeds and I taxied out ahead of the others. Typical of the time of year, the temperatures dropped near freezing at night, so I hesitated a few minutes to tickle up the engine temperature. Suddenly, Hoover taxied out around me and shot down the runway with the cold engine popping. He pulled the Spit off as the gear was retracting and began to slow roll (rolling the plane smoothly around on its forward moving axis as it continues through inverted and back around to upright position). He had, what any reasonable pilot would surmise, as inadequate airspeed to complete the roll before he went home in a box. But since Hoover was not just any reasonable pilot, he completed the roll grazing some scrub brush with his wing tip just beyond the end of the runway.

When I got the flight home I collared Hoover and remarked, "Damn, Hoover, you've gotta be the best damned pilot I've ever seen. But damn it man if you're not going to bust your butt with stupid crap like you pulled back there at Tunis."

"God, yea, Mac," Hoover began. "You know ... I ... ah ... forgot I had mah toilet kit a-sittin' on mah lap. The God damned thing fell raht in front of mah face ... and I ... ah ... couldn't see a thang."

It's easy to see how prophetic I was. Hoover spent a lifetime racking up thousands of hours in handling some of the riskiest test pilot duties and death-defying air show feats conceivable. Today in his 80's, Hoover is still doing his thang. He continues to dazzle audiences in his P–51 Mustang, F–86 Saberjet, and others.

Anybody Seen the War?

To recap the general military situation in the theater, British General Bernard Montgomery had encountered hard fighting in eastern Sicily and had engaged in some publicized ego skirmishes with Patton in western Sicily. Together, their troops eventually forced the German evacuation across the Straits of Messina.

The Germans had been cornered in Messina with their backs to the water, but they still managed to ship, air-lift, and barge most of their men and equipment across the straits and into southern Italy. The 52nd was not summoned to hinder the beleaguered Nazis.

In early September 1943, the British crossed the straits and invaded the Italian toe. Within days, U.S. General Mark Clark's 5th Army landed up the boot at two points in the gulf of Salerno, fifty miles below Naples. The Germans expected the Allied landing and reacted swiftly and vigorously. With the beachheads in doubt, every available airplane in the Mediterranean Theater was sent in including carrier forces ... that is, except us. Strangely, the 52nd was still ordained to cruise over the convoys without participating. However, that ensuing bombardment proved effective. This effort, along with the landing of tanks and a rendezvous with the British coming up from the south, soon sent the enemy into a retreat northward. Moreover, it allowed the Western Allies their first firm foothold on the European continent, and what better place to have a foothold than on the Italian boot?

The frustrating news, was that after almost seven months of flying fighter planes in a World War II war zone I had not fired a shot in combat. The question of the continuing failure of leadership to employ at critical junctures, certain needed, readily available resources, such as our 52nd Fighter Group, remains an unanswered mystery. In early December 1943, following my recovery from yellow jaundice, we bid farewell to Palermo and flew the Spits to Corsica. Were the winds of war finally blowing our direction?

Chapter 8

Found the War

Napoleon's and My Corsica — 1944

Corsica was a jewel of an island and Calvi, our Corsican duty spot, was certainly a fine point in the cutting. On display in our family room today is a travel poster of Calvi showing a cruise ship pulling into the harbor. It's still being guarded by the magnificent, but ancient and decaying, Citadel rising off high cliffs at its harbor entrance. In May of 1981, I revisited Corsica with my wife, Lois and our dear friends Doug and Heather Campbell. What a nostalgic trip that was.

For me, Corsica was a continuation of the Alps with pine forests, ski resorts and quaint villages. It is the third largest island in the western Mediterranean and is separated from the mainland Alps by a hundred miles or so of sea. It is roughly 115 miles long and about 50 miles across. But it is much more. Most of the coastal topography is sheer rocky cliffs, like our California Big Sur coastline. In the occasional breaks, picturesque harbor towns and cities languish, uniquely remote from mainland Europe. There also are a few flatlands between the mountains and the sea where farming and livestock grazing flourish. At its narrowest crossing it is only about 100 sea miles between Calvi and the French and Italian Riviera coasts.

A Friendly Stuka Dive Bomber?

Flying the Spits from Palermo, Sicily to Corsica entailed a 250 mile first leg over water flight to Cagliari, the capital port city of the Island of Sardinia. For some reason, instead of making the trip as a squadron, we flew in separate two-plane units. McCauley and I flew as a pair. We were to stop for refueling at an airport near Cagliari occupied by B–26s (U.S. medium bombers). As we began circling the area looking for the field, I couldn't believe my eyes when I spotted a lone JU–87 Stuka dive-bomber about two miles ahead and slightly below us. McCauley scooted his Spit alongside mine and pointed wildly.

After a terse, excited radio discussion, we armed our guns and made for the Stuka with juices surging. I got within firing range before I noticed the absence of rear cockpit guns and then, would you believe, a big American star insignia on the wings. I shouted to McCauley and broke off just as he saw the same sight. We followed the Stuka in to the American airfield at Cagliari and parked nearby. Two American pilots met us along side the Stuka, which was their toy. McCauley advised them it was a dangerous one with virgin fighter guys like us around.

Land There? Course I Can!

We then flew north, for another hundred miles or so across the straits separating Sardinia and the island of Corsica without incident. Another breathtakingly beautiful stretch of about hundred miles and we prepared to land at our new harbor home, Calvi, on the northwestern corner of Corsica. As we arrived, our immediate concern was the sight of two grass runways, which turned out to be 2000 and 1800 feet long. Throwing in some nearby hills added to the challenge. The B–26 bombers flying out of our previous stopover at Cagliari had over 4000 feet. Gross discrimination! McCauley and I plunked down with room to spare.

A Bleak December

Our flight surgeon, Doc Curran, kept me on the ground for the month of December 1943. I was weak from my illness and needed to gain weight. The rest of the guys however, were slowly beginning to taste combat. The weather was cold and wet and the runways were puddled and rutted. This made combat indoctrination doubly troubling. Missions were few and small, runway accidents were many.

On December 7th, Tim Tyler and Will LaBarge scrambled two Spits and chased a Messerschmitt 210 airplane in and out of the clouds. Tim finally knocked it down only twenty miles southeast of Calvi. LaBarge, on landing, totaled his Spit on the muddy runway. He had to be extracted, but was not seriously hurt.

On December 8th, Captain Lee Towbridge, soon to be our new commanding officer, showed us a new way to capture an enemy flag. The captain had been leading a strafing flight against troops, trucks and trains along the Italian Riviera. Flying quite low, his right wing struck an unseen, three-inch steel flagpole. The thing penetrated like a huge dull, knife cutting into the wing root for about two feet. The pole miraculously tore from its base as it stopped at the wing's main spar and wrapped around the Spit's wing like a giant hairpin.

Upon Trowbridge's harrowing return, the "hairpin" portion trailing under the wing blocked his attempt to lower the Spit's wheels. Accordingly, he was forced to belly-land his bird and its new attachment on our Calvi nesting place runway. Several of us breathlessly watched Trow's approach to the field sporting the unbelievable, unrecognizable, non-flying object. We cheered with relief as he hopped safely out of his pane's remains following a rough slide to a stop on the grass. How that good-old Spit had held onto its wing at all, or how the plane had not been tossed uncontrollably into the landscape, left us all looking up to a deceivingly empty sky.

Spitfire and Trowbridge take flagpole home
Photo courtesy of Bob McCampbell

More bad weather and bad luck were perhaps the reasons for Hugh Dorland's fatal crash on December 19th. Poor visibility and runway problems brought him down soon after takeoff.

McCauley returning on his first mission, a fighter sweep over Southern France, escaped serious injury when his plane hit a rut on the runway, completely destroying his airplane.

During late December, Doc Curran lengthened my leash, allowing me to keep my hand in for a few training hops including some practice dive bombing runs. Fortunately, with deadly aim, I managed to hit the Mediterranean Sea. Finally, thanks to a visit by some sailors and their LST craft full of goodies, all of the squadron's officers and men were treated to a magnificent Christmas feast.

First Combat Mission – Shooting at Me Personally?

May through December 1943 had brought us no combat experience. On New Year's Day, 1944 McCauley and I were scrambled to chase a reconnaissance, twin-engine, Messerschmitt 210. Germans had most likely removed armor plating and most weapons to increase speed because the adversary held his distance from us until he was back over the French coast. Low fuel forced us to return.

On January 2, I was firing at the enemy and he was firing back! I was assigned to fly Smitty's wing on a two-man sweep to the Italian port of Savona, and down the Riviera toward Nice, for a "look see." Smitty, an ex-Harvard and RAF guy, was old by my orientation. After all, he was almost thirty, but as eager to "fight the Hun" as anyone I'd ever encountered. He was smart, but a loner, and certainly not the stereotypical Harvard man. He'd been kicked out of prewar Army Air Corps Cadet Training for, as he characterized it, social reasons. Smitty was a bit profane and only barely mannered otherwise. I couldn't help liking him, nonetheless. He was a good friend and one I had confidence in.

Before we climbed into the cockpit Smitty gave me a mini-briefing. "Mac, we want to stay under the radar all the way in. You stay with me, right on the water. And keep your head on a swivel." *How the hell am I going to hold a Spit ten or twenty feet above the water for one hundred plus miles and keep my head on a swivel?*

Shortly after takeoff, with me in tow, Smitty poked his nose as close to the water as possible without getting wet and stayed there the entire trip. Sea spray occasionally splashed my windscreen. Worse yet, continuously measuring my distance from the water gave me vertigo!

Smitty navigated us perfectly to Savona Harbor. Suddenly, he yelled, "Arm your guns, Mac, and go for it!" He pulled up abruptly to provide an adequate firing trajectory, and I stuck with him as he let an ocean-going tug have it broadside with cannon. I broke away toward a second tug and hit it at the water line ... blowing its boiler!

"Mac, you sweep your side of the docks and I'll sweep mine," Smitty added. "Then stick your nose down and head home."

Before bugging out, I torched a military truck and trailer, messed up a warehouse, and scattered a gun emplacement crew. I was relieved when we safely poked our noses back down on the water and headed home without being hit. Small and heavy caliber weapons fired at us from the periphery of the harbor but thank God the enemy's aim was atrocious! The heavy anti-aircraft guns had been firing at an empty sky for most of our intrusion, but some machine gun and other small caliber fire had come closer. As the tracers danced around us, I had my first (not the last) frightening realization that someone was actually trying to kill me ... me in particular!

Me Again?

On a cold misty morning early in January, several of us were sitting around a table in the mess, shooting the bull over a brace of coffee. We were abruptly interrupted as the CO, Capt.. Sam Houston, returned from the airfield, poured himself a short cup and looked directly at me.

"Mac, Brown's flight is just back and they've seen a large armed merchant ship trying to slip along the coast under the weather. They lost him in the stuff before they could strafe him. Lets you and me see if we can find him ... with a couple of bombs."

A few weeks before, Captain Sam and Tim Tyler had flown down to a British Spit group in Malta to have bomb racks installed on their Spitfires. Within a week most our planes had racks and we'd stocked a bomb dump with a few dozen 250 pounders. Most of us pilots weren't exactly wild about dive-bombing so we drew straws to see who got to do an inaugural practice drop on some off shore rocks. I won and once again managed to hit the Mediterranean Sea.

250 lb high explosive bomb

Spitfire loaded with bombs
Photo courtesy of Bob McCampbell

I should also mention that for several reasons Spitfires were not well suited for dive-bombing. And that is probably one reason you will find little reference to such usage anywhere but here. To be at all accurate you had to release bombs from a dead vertical dive at the target. The Spit just didn't like to do that. It just wanted to get its nose back up. Also without dive flaps, (such as the German Stuka and the U.S. Navy Dauntless dive-bombers had) any fighter moved too fast vertically for best dive-bombing results. A dive-bomber, slowed by flaps, could hold its vertical attitude closer to its target before pull out. Still, some conventional fighters on both sides did score some amazing hits.

A driver jeeped Captain Sam and me out to our airfield a few miles away. The planes were already armed and warmed up. I was not sure I was. We jumped in our birds, taxied out and with a thumbs up from the Skipper we rolled down and off the turf with a load of high explosives. We flew low across the rather rough sea until we were a few miles from the French coast.

We were in and out of clouds as we climbed to about ten thousand feet searching for the ship. We figured that if the vessel maintained her course in the time since she was last spotted we'd find her somewhere not far off shore a few miles northwest of Nice. We were not to be disappointed because just as I was calculating our remaining search time, the Skipper transmitted, "Thar she blows." Sure enough through a break in the clouds we spotted the large freighter. It was apparently trying to make it under winter weather with goodies for the "Huns" who were manning the stalemate on the Italian front.

The Skipper outlined an approach plan, then yelled "Tally Ho", as he rolled on his back and pulled the bird through to vertical. In about 10 seconds, I followed him, trying to hold the nose on the prey, while trying to watch him and my altimeter. I released my bombs at about 3,000 feet and I could see flak from aft-mounted 40 mm anti-air weapons and from low altitude 20 mm cannon throughout my dive. The enemy fire continued as I recovered low over the water. "You were close, Mac," said the Skipper as I finally spotted him circling ahead of me. "Let's hit the road."

Unfortunately we missed the target but I was glad to be returning. The weather was deteriorating and a cold rain on the windscreen wasn't helping the visibility. Then, about 30 miles out, the Skipper called the ready room back at the base. "I want crews ready to rearm and turn us around when we touch down. It's gotta be fast."

It was like an Indy 500 pit stop. The crews were all over our birds when we taxied in. A refueling truck was there by the time we switched off engines followed closely by a Jeep and bomb trailer. We dismounted, ran into the ready shack for a personal pit stop and were back into the wild blue yonder to try again.

As one might have guessed my heart had skipped a couple of beats when the Skipper announced his version of John Paul Jones' "We've not yet begun to fight." I envisioned fifty enemy fighters awaiting our arrival, and much more alert shipboard gunners for this second time around. Nevertheless, we found the ship again and began the routine in the same way as before. This time the ships' gunners began firing earlier like the crowd of intimidators facing an NBA free thrower. So far no 109s and down went the Skipper and down went I, watching the cannon muzzles blinking all the way. I had hesitated a little longer this time and was far enough behind to see the Skipper's bombs splash to starboard as I began my dive.

I had missed to starboard on the first run and I corrected to port in an instant. I was too busy pulling out to see my bombs hit, but the Skipper had made a tight turn over the water and had seen my results. He excitedly called to congratulate me on shaving the ship with a bomb along the starboard side and likely, mortally wounding her below the waterline. Later he had said that our small bombs probably wouldn't have done nearly as much damage had we scored a direct hit. The next day we learned that the ship had run for Nice harbor and wound up there partially capsized at dockside. Mission accomplished.

Our Own Little War

From that first combat mission until the end of January 1944, I flew twenty-four more missions, with a similar number in February. Oddly, I never knew what our mission objectives and directions were or from which authority they originated. But there was no mistake that our little squadron was waging its own private war against occupied Europe along the French and Italian Rivieras.

We even became celebrities of sorts on the German side. We had a good short wave radio in our bar that picked up a wide range of European broadcasts. The universal language of music provided welcome entertainment on cold nights. We regularly turned to German radio, especially the German propaganda broadcasts of Axis Sally and her selection of American popular music. Axis Sally tried to sound like a combination of the American girl next door and a come-hither seductress. Sally told us how bad the war was going for us and how the wealthy Jews back home were making out with our wives and sweethearts. But one evening after a return from a dive bombing run, we were startled to hear her usual sweet talk turn into a stern admonishment of our little squadron and its foul deeds.

"Now, you boys flying the Spitfires from Corsica should be ashamed of your continuing and heartless destruction of the lives of innocent children and priceless art treasures along the Riviera. You, I'm sorry to say, will be promptly and severely dealt with."

I guess she wasn't kidding. Within a few days, a squadron of Focke-Wulf 190s moved into the vicinity of our playground.

Worn Sheet Music

A hit tune in Germany, and amongst the troops of all nations at the time, had been *Lilly Marlene*. It was a simple, but haunting melody about a young Fräulein waiting under a street corner lantern for the promised return of her soldier boy; a worn promise apparently never to be fulfilled. I played that tune on the guitar for years, singing it with the German lyrics, and inevitably, shedding a tear for all the loving people of all nations whose soldiers never returned.

Worn Pages and Memories

Each day included operational flying. On one day I actually flew three missions, two combat and one sad, unsuccessful search off the French coast for a downed buddy. According to the one-inch remarks column in my flight log sheet, a typical mission included either a fighter sweep or dive bomb or recon (for reconnaissance) or flying escort for B–25s. We flew two-to-four plane missions, and on a rare occasion, a six-plane escort run. Ordinarily, we strafed military supply convoys and troop trains bound for the front. We also attacked coastal gun emplacements and radar sights, and dive-bombed shipping and petroleum storage facilities. On a few such missions we were attacked by enemy fighters, and too often, came out second best. Over the three months of Spitfire combat action, our squadron lost almost two-thirds of its pilots, mainly to antiaircraft fire and accidents. These losses were tough on our small close-knit bunch.

Worn Aircraft

The Spitfire MK–5 was a 1940, Battle of Britain vintage machine modified to accommodate two wing-mounted 20 mm cannons. During WWI and WWII, new and modified airplanes were being introduced every few months. The latest enemy fighters, such as the ME–109 G6, were a good 70 mph faster than the German and RAF fighters of fall 1940. They were clearly superior to our Spits in both speed and rate of climb. We could out-turn them, but we also had the disadvantage of less range; (two hours at most using higher power settings). The Germans shared the same range disadvantage, but they were working a lot closer to home.

Worn to Keep Warm

The winter of '44 was unusually cold for Southern Europe and a couple of snows covered our island right down to the waterfront. The Spitfire was a cold airplane to play war in. I joked that the British were more acclimated to cold than us Southern California pilots. We tried several combinations of clothing but each pilot wound up with his own solution. Generally we found the U.S. gear warm enough but too heavy and cumbersome for the needed flexibility in the small fighter cockpit. Most of us found several layers of thinner clothing the most satisfactory arrangement. I wore long johns, khaki pants and shirt, a sweatshirt, flight coveralls and a thin leather jacket. Likewise we found the thin, limey (RAF issue) leather gloves with silk liners preferable to the bulky U.S. fleece-lined ones. Some missions were so cold that I still alternated hands between the stick and my crotch in order to keep one warm.

Warmed by 130 – Octane

Most of the squadron officers lived at the Hotel Bonaparte in downtown Calvi. It was a two-story lodge with about a dozen rooms and adequate space for our bar and officers mess on the bottom floor. Six of us were billeted in a nice residence within easy walking distance from the hotel. Depending on room size, two or three pilots shared a room. McCauley, Ellis and I set up a relatively comfortable three cot, two desk, one heater suite overlooking a garden. Sadly, Ellis was lost on a mission over northern Italy in February 1944.

Down the hall, two of our pilots occupied a bridal suite with one, Stan Pell, nesting in a massive canopy bed. This accommodation naturally generated endless squadron taunts, jokes and jibes.

Since few of the residential hotel rooms had any heating, we engineered our own gasoline drip heaters. Simply stated, ours consisted of a jerry can of 130–octane aviation fuel sitting on the floor with siphoned gas rising through copper tubing that dripped down on some rocks in a potbellied-like stove. A petcock on the tubing controlled the gas flow and the fumes were fed out a windowpane through a stove-pipe that rounded out the Rube Goldberg arrangement. The pipe at first startled the locals, some of whom mistook it for an American anti aircraft weapon. It took the chill off on the coldest nights but not without some close calls with petrol fires.

We were awakened one night to shouts of "Fire! Fire! Fire!" I jumped out of bed as Pell hollered "Grab some water, Mac! It's a hot time in the bridal suite tonight!" McCauley grabbed a heavy, old-fashioned fire extinguisher taken from the flight line for just such an occasion and I ran with an Army blanket. The bridal bed canopy was pretty well engulfed. Thankfully we were able to douse it before the gas-can exploded. Luckily, there was no structural damage, just a scarred and violated bridal suite. Most evenings, except for sleeping, we preferred to warm our cold hearts at a favorite bar on the waterfront. Billiards in the back room kept most of us off the streets.

More Drop Drama

Our dive-bombing missions during January, February and March of '44 were always a little hair-raising, fighting to keep the Spit under control in the vertical dive. My gut still churns from a close one I had on a mission to hit some large petroleum storage tanks near Savona harbor on the Italian Riviera. There were six of us, stacked in echelon (like geese) over the target. I was number five in the formation. The squadron leader called "tally ho" and rolled over and down toward the target. The flak was flying at him and around us as we waited our turn.

As I began my dive, I could see a couple of good hits and explosions and the problem for me was to aim at something that wasn't already done in. What we'd found of advantage in holding the nose vertical was to roll the elevator trim tab forward just before the dive. This placed the plane in a nose heavy mode or mood if you prefer and necessitated heavy back pull on the stick to keep the plane in level flight.

With little coaxing, the Spit would anxiously move into a vertical dive and contentedly stay there until either one of three things happened: the pilot used both hands and all of his strength on the stick to pull out; he let go with his left hand and tried (quick as hell!) to roll the trim tab wheel back to level position; or he dug a deep, fiery hole and final resting place in foreign ground.

On this day, I hit my target... a couple of large petrol tanks exploded in flames ... Great. *Let's get out of here! Dammed! This thing doesn't want to pull out... And it's corkscrewed itself ... Shhhhhhh ... come on Baby!* I was frantically trying options "one" and "two" and was terrifyingly headed for success in "three." I finally got the nose up, dodged a tall crane, and then cranked a tight turn to miss a hillside. Instead of pulling out of the bomb run going away from the target area, I found myself narrowly hedge hopping over the harbor and its defenses.

I thought, *God, now that you've saved me from the deep hole, Please don't give the Huns a skeet shoot!* Inadvertently, I sailed right over gun emplacements scattering people in all directions. I cranked a shuddering tight turn, pushed the nose below the taller buildings and headed out to sea, waiting for the worst from behind. Ground fire had been relatively heavy before and during my dive, but now it had stopped altogether. It resumed briefly after I was out of range and tickling the waves toward home.

My Airplane is Bent

The old Spit I had been flying for the past few missions had been the first airplane assigned to me as my very own. The good news was that within limits, I could personalize its external appearance with my name, its name, aerial victories, and maybe some nose art. Unlike an auto, the flying characteristics of each identically manufactured airplane varied. On older planes that had been rode hard through rough pastures, the handling could differ in significant ways.

The bad news was that my airplane was a bit of a dog. But like some of my real best friends, it was mine and I hated to part with it. After my wild dive-bombing ride, I complained to my dedicated, innovative crew chief, Fred Wiersma, about my Spit's corkscrew problem. Fred brilliantly responded with his trusty pliers and eyeballed an upward bend in the fixed trim tab on the right aileron. The older Spits had lacked a pilot-adjustable aileron trim system. With Fred's interpretive insight into my complaint, his all-around airplane maintenance genius and devilish dexterity with pliers, the problem was solved. Eat your heart out you modern, high-tech engineers!

Heroic Ace ... Tragic Loss

I can't, in good conscience, depart from a discussion of my strained love affair with my old Spit, WD–D, without a tribute to its original master.

Lt. Sylvan Feld, Top Spitfire Ace
Photo courtesy of Bob McCampbell

First Lt. Sylvan Feld, was the top scoring Spitfire ace in the North African campaign. Feld downed nine German planes in a little over two months of combat action. This record is even more remarkable when one considers the setting in which he did it. North Africa had become the baptismal American war effort against the seasoned Axis forces of Western Europe. Green airmen and ground forces alike suffered the toughest of learning curves, set-backs and losses before finally prevailing.

Lt. Feld had transferred from our 4th Squadron to a P–47 Thunderbolt outfit in England as we were signing on to the 4th in June 1943. In due time I was to inherit his well-known Spit. Regrettably, his Thunderbolt fighter was downed by enemy anti-aircraft fire in August 1944. Ironically, as a German prisoner, he was killed one month later in an Allied air raid. I can only add that Sylvan Feld, God bless him, wrung the best out of our mutual chariot.

Gone Fishing

First let me say, nothing is more important than food in any environment. Secondly let me offer that dive-bombing also has its place at the table. In Italy we were fed well considering the circumstances. On Christmas and Thanksgiving, tons of turkeys were shipped into Sicily and Corsica. How the U.S. military ocean-shipped, preserved and so widely distributed the sacred birds for timely arrival at the scattered military units around the world remains a logistics miracle to me. Only in the most desperate, isolated circumstances did the American Army of WWII ever go hungry. A food-bearing LST (Landing Ship, Tank) always showed up in time at the remotest island in the South Pacific or to ours on the worlds other side.

Still, we griped about the food. The poor army cooks did the best they could with the limited and repetitive range of canned meat, beans and vegetables. Sometimes the food was over-productive of gas as stomachs expanded at high altitudes. We did learn to avoid beans prior to certain flying schedules. Occasionally, we pilots experimented in the kitchen. We deep-fried Spam, potatoes and other canned foods and added local spices, herbs and home-made sauces. Some of the guys were fairly innovative cooks. We also foraged at times, bartering with a local farmer for a sheep or pig. In spite of the major improvement in meals occasioned by this sort of quartermastering, we reluctantly gave up the meat procurement business when we realized how desperately the locals needed the food for themselves.

One night after shooting snooker pool at a bistro along the waterfront, McCauley, Bullock, Tribbett and I acquainted ourselves with the British captain of a small Royal Navy patrol boat. The boat and its six-man crew were berthed at the Calvi harbor serving as our air/sea rescue support. The Skipper, appropriately named Reggie, was a jolly, middle-aged former yachtsman who maintained his own small captain's lounge on the patrol boat. Here, two or three of us were frequently treated to his wine and regaled by his inexhaustible repertoire of factual, fanciful and humorous bits of British history. His delightful lectures were spiced with the tales of debauchery, treachery and buffoonery of British royalty and high society. They must have been the fountainhead of the incomparable British limericks we became so fond of.

Reggie had a five-gallon water bottle dispenser always filled with his favorite semi-sweet vermouth. A Dixie cup holder was attached. It was Reggie who offered that the waters off Calvi were a graduate school of a limited number of very delectable fish. He followed up by advising that at the time of our practice bomb runs off the coast, he and his crew ventured out and found a wide circle of stunned fish on the surface. It seemed Reggie and his boys took a dinghy and a fish net and selectively landed a gourmet seafood dinner.

The die was cast without casting. I think it was the very next day that McCauley made a practice dive bomb run. With watches synchronized, Captain Reggie's boat was in the lead followed by two borrowed outboard skiffs, crewed by a few of our squadron guys. Together we netted enough good fish to feed all the 200 officers and men of our 4th Squadron. This resultant fish fry also reefed in a festive spirit of camaraderie amongst us all. Such an all-unit party in our wartime environment was notably rare. As a meal, the fish catch was a delicious rare treat in itself. Couldn't really say the same for the vintage value of the locally procured wine, but who cared?

Chapter 9

Victory Won — Friend & Gal Lost

Wo Sint Das Luftwaffe?

Where were the enemy fighters in our Mediterranean fly zone? By March of 1944 the Luftwaffe was beginning to be strung out a bit thin. The Russian front was now a high priority and was sapping German air resources. But most importantly, the intensifying strategic strikes by the American long-range bomber forces from England and Southern Italy were beginning to exact a toll that demanded a concentration of air defences over Central Europe.

Night v. Day Bombing

The history of American strategic air operations in WWII Europe unfolds a tale of frustration and eventual success. As the American buildup of heavy bombers and other aircraft had begun to swell in 1943, the British and American air staffs differed on how best to conduct long-range bombing operations. The British adamantly preferred night raids which experience had shown them was the only way to go.

Initial RAF efforts at daylight raids, even without deep territorial penetration had proven too costly. The Americans argued that they could be more accurate and effective against strategic targets in the daytime. The British countered that once the daytime bombers were beyond the range of fighter escorts they were too vulnerable to the German fighters.

The Americans wouldn't have any of the British concerns and offered that their B-17 and B-24 heavy bombers were so heavily armed they could take care of themselves. After all, B-17s were not named Flying Fortresses for nothing.

Unfortunately, as American strategic air operations progressed and bombers began reaching beyond the range of their escorting fighters, losses got heavier. In fact losses were beginning to become unacceptable. For example, in one raid in late 1943 on the industrial centers at Regensburg and Schweinfurt, 70 Fortress heavy bombers and 700 crew members were lost. More than 100 bombers were badly damaged and scores of their crewmen dead or injured. The problem was getting down to the question of, "How many more raids can we launch before we run out of airplanes and crews?"

That dilemma left the American commanding generals in an embarrassing, if not desperate position. Eureka! The amazing and timely solution arrived in a small package of dynamite called the Mustang. This American fighter with a newly adopted British Rolls Royce engine was the answer to a general's prayer. The P-51B Mustang could fly farther, faster and better than anything in the field. Its introduction in late 1943, meant fighters could accompany bombers all the way. As a result, the losses of bombers and their crews declined and the war was inevitably shortened.

System of Survival

The Luftwaffe was not always absent in our playground. Once in a while we'd do enough damage to get their attention.

The ME-109s and the FW-190s would commonly attack from above and out of the sun. They would squirt a burst of fire when in range and use their extra zoom to smartly climb back up for another go at it. They would rarely stay down and tangle or dog fight. As a result our tactics were commonly defensive ones, hoping to see them early on in their attack.

A substantial proportion of aerial victories on both sides were scored against adversaries who never saw the attacker coming. Things happened in a moment after tedious hours, even weeks, of no sightings. You had to keep your head on a swivel. There were so many things to look at ... formation flying, instruments, navigation points, and friendly planes. A flyspeck on the canopy could prove startling.

Luftwaffe—Taught Tactics

Much of the aerial fighting in WWI seemed to have disintegrated into an every man for himself business. Between the wars, our country's military (flying) formations and those of most of other countries were done in tight, pretty, crowd-pleasing echelons. The German Luftwaffe, in the mid 1930s and while participating in the Spanish Civil War, had adopted some major changes in fighter tactics. Unfolding out of the war in Spain were some surprisingly sizable aerial actions. These mainly pitted volunteer Russian and German pilots and planes against one another, in a pre-WWII warm-up game.

In Spain, it quickly dawned on the Germans that tight, pretty formations were unwieldy in combat. Especially at the higher speeds and wider turning radiuses of their new Messerschmitts, a looser pattern afforded more flexibility in offense and defense. The RAF pilots in their first WWII encounters with the Luftwaffe fighters were aghast at finding what appeared to be a disorderly hoard of enemy planes hurling themselves into battle. The Brits soon realized that the peacetime parade formations were unhealthy to a flying career. Moreover, they found that the Germans did indeed have a systematic order in their madness and an effective one.

As we Americans arrived, we were tutored, luckily, by the RAF chaps. We learned to fly a finger four, or box formation, where each pilot had a particular area or visual zone responsibility. The finger four was a loose, flexible one whereby the element leader (#3) could roam to either side of the flight leader (#1). The wingmen (#2 & 4) could move to the inside of their turning lead plane. The flight leader with his four planes and the squadron leader with perhaps 16 (4 flights) could thus turn without leaving his squadron mates behind. When his leader turned, each pilot, accommodated by the flexibility of the finger formation, could scoot underneath and to the inside of the turn.

Clock Works

Each pilot sat in the middle of an imaginary horizontal clock with 12 o'clock dead ahead and 6 o'clock directly behind. Nine o'clock and three o'clock were directly left and directly right respectively. Each pilot had a specific quadrant on which to concentrate. Looking to his right the flight leader in this diagram covered the 45 degree quadrant from 12 to 3 o'clock. His wingman covered the 3 to 6 o'clock quadrant to his right. Likewise, the element leader and his wingman covered the two quadrants to the left, completing the circle. The zones of responsibility switch directions whenever turns and other maneuvers mandate an element to position itself on the opposite or 9 o'clock side of the flight leader.

An omission in our stateside training had been the lack of emphasis on something as basic as clock orientation. When we had first arrived in the squadron, Smitty had insisted on drilling us on any occasion. Walking down the street, or anywhere with Smitty, he would call out, "Bandit at 4 o'clock high" and we would snap our necks in the direction of the oncom-

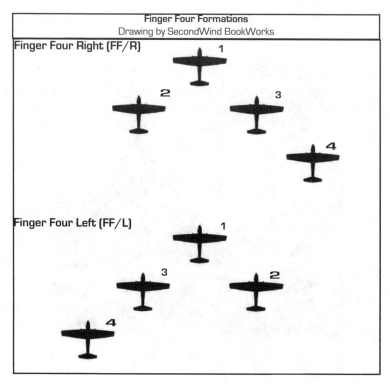

Finger Four Formations
Drawing by SecondWind BookWorks

Finger Four Right (FF/R)

1

2

3

4

Finger Four Left (FF/L)

1

3

2

4

ing enemy. It didn't take long to shorten the precious microseconds between his call and our reactions.

On the Clock

Only once while flying Spits was I jumped by enemy fighters. Our flight of four was just reforming from the scatter of a dive-bombing run. We were only a few thousand feet above the sea and a call "Bogies at 5 o'clock high" rang out. The excitement blossomed, then exploded as my lead ship's wingman and others began interrupting, "They're Bandits! 6 o'clock" ... "They're coming in!" ... "Get ready to break!"

A "break" was a defensive procedure used against opposing fighters who were attacking from above and behind and at greater speed. We would wait until the attacker was almost in firing range and

A tired old WD-D. But it was mine!
Photo courtesy of Bob McCampbell

then quickly turn the slower moving defending plane directly toward the oncoming attacker. This turn was done as tightly as possible. Ideally timed, this forced the faster moving attacker into a wider turn and outside the smaller arc available to his slower adversary. It could also create a head-on encounter, which was a dangerous but at least an equal opportunity event.

The attacking planes were four ME–109 G6 types. I caught sight of two of them boring in toward me from above and about 5 o'clock. My heart was beating louder than the Merlin engine of my Spitfire.

"Tackle Red 3 and 4, ready to break ... break right ... now!" Called Canning, the flight leader.

While pulling the stick tight into my gut I shouted, "Tackle Red 1 ... 2, Bandits from 7 o'clock. Break left ... now!"

I had seen the other two 109's closing on Canning just as my element leader and I were breaking into the first attackers.

The breaks worked as the 109's wasted some ammo and skidded by outside our turning arcs. I wasted some ammo too, squeezing off a couple of cannon bursts after a sharply climbing 109, which was just out of range. Typically, the adversaries didn't linger to tangle and zoomed back up with their speed advantage to take another crack at us.

Friendly Clouds

Playing this kind of dodge-ball against skilled pilots with planes of superior performance, likely wouldn't work forever. Our fuel was limited too. We reformed our box in the direction of Corsica and watched for the next assault. We could see it coming when Canning said, "Poke your noses down through the cloud cover on the deck, and throttle to the wall."

The 109's were gaining on us but we were tough to catch diving all out for the cloud layer and the deck. If they challenged us low and under the clouds, odds were that we'd be on a level playing field. We circled below the cloud layer for a bit, hoping the attackers would try to mix it up with us there. No luck. We then followed Canning and poked our noses back above the cloud layer for a look. The enemy's fuel levels may have become a concern or they simply opted against tangling with us on our terms. They had vanished. A half-hour later, I was happy to see our runway. I think we all felt a little cowardly at having initially run for cloud cover.

Eyes of the Beholder

Bob Hoover and three other squadron mates got into a similar situation with enemy fighters just a few days later. Sadly, the results were much more unforgiving and certainly more controversial. The flight had just completed a dive-bombing run on a ship convoy. It was Hoover's first encounter with enemy fighters, and ironically, his last. The flight of four was led by Flight Officer "Monty" Montgomery, with his wingman, 1st Lt. Hank Montgomery. It also included Flight Officer Bob Hoover as element leader and his wingman 2nd Lt. "Smitty" Smith.

The four Spits had become typically scattered while recovering from a dive-bombing run. The Flight Leader, Montgomery was shot down by an enemy fighter and killed as he pulled out of his bomb run. Bob Hoover was downed soon thereafter. The two returning pilots brought back word that Hoover had tried to "take on the whole Luftwaffe alone."

The survivors, Smitty and Hank had been in quite a melee themselves. A Focke-Wulf 190 fighter had hit Hank's Spit. It would be many years later that I was stunned to read in Hoover's book, *Forever Flying*, his accusation that his flight mates had abandoned him when he was shot down. This certainly hit me as a serious charge and a disappointing one.

You can imagine my anxious curiosity when a March 2000 issue of *Aviation History* magazine featured an article on the incident. To my surprise, the author was none other than Bob Curtis, former commanding officer of our group's 2nd Squadron and one of the 52nd Group's most respected combat leaders. With his amazing tally of 14 aerial victories, he became one of Europe's leading American aces. I had known Bob Curtis only sparingly overseas. Most of that had amounted to brief intercoms between us during a couple of combat missions. We later became more closely acquainted when we were later assigned to the same stateside command. Bob Curtis clearly did an enviable job of investigative reporting and analysis of Hoover's infamous, gut-wrenching and controversial combat incident.

That Hoover had been shot down and taken prisoner for the balance of the war was indisputable. It was also clear that the flight leader, Monty Montgomery, bombed first, and as he pulled out from his run, was first to be attacked. Also, there was little question that typically the flight's dive-bombers became somewhat dispersed coming out of their dive run. Finally, it's clear that before regrouping, all four Spits were attacked or engaged against superior performing enemy planes.

Curtis' article covers in detail Hank's and Smitty's individual combat reports and Hoover's postwar book statements on the mission. Then he summarizes "I believe that Hoover was right to feel all alone because he was ... but not because he had been abandoned." Curtis also relates that Hank, the second to bomb, was also the second to be engaged with and damaged by the enemy. While Hoover, the third in the bomb run, was pulling out, he congratulated Smitty, the fourth bomber, for having hit the target. Moments later, Hoover became heavily engaged with two or three of the Focke-Wulfs. Smitty, as he pulled out, saw Hoover jousting with the enemy and climbed all-out toward him. As he proceeded, Smitty was distracted and engaged a nearby diving Focke-Wulf. Curtis adds that "Smith can be faulted for that, but it is impossible to know whether he could have rejoined Hoover in time to be of any help."

Curtis concludes, "Although Hoover did not, as he claimed, shoot down one of the 190s, he nevertheless performed well in his first engagement with enemy fighters. Still, I feel he let his emotions get the better of him when he accused those two pilots of abandoning him, especially since his statement that 'the two deserters were chastened severely when they later returned to safety', implies that they simply fled the scene. Montgomery's and Smith's combat reports show they did neither, and nothing for which they would have been chastised."

I must add that Bob Curtis' credentials are considered impeccable by his wartime and lifetime superiors, peers and subordinates. As for Smitty, I knew him well in the wartime skies and on the ground and he was no coward ... his very reason for being was to destroy the enemy. If anything, he bordered on recklessness in his quest. Yes, we did joke and even sing about such topics as "You get in trouble up there again and I'm out of there." But, in reality I never experienced any such act of cowardice in combat. There's no doubt wrong decisions were made, especially in combat situations, even by generals. Perhaps one of those happened on this mission. And yes, there were, no doubt, some of us who were more fearful than others. But as an old friend and ex-Navy combat pilot put it the other day, "There should be a special medal for us more fearful of combat than most because we still, and without hesitation, just went ahead and did it anyway."

Hoover must have had far more guts than most or he never could have flown the thousands of incomparable performances he's done for presidents, kings, peers and public. Hoover's flying skills paralleled those of the great athletes of other sports. He could fly an airplane, any airplane, and feel the thresholds of its flying limits. He could appropriately interact with the plane as though it was an integrated appendage of his body. Hoover reinforced the theory that "The whole is something greater than the sum of its parts."

I think, in Hoover's case, the resulting whole was a bird. All of us who passed his way have expressed words to the effect "But for a folly of fate, Hoover could have been one of the greatest wartime fighter pilots ever." I must also add that Hoover was a well-liked and respected comrade. So Bob Hoover was human. As such and under the circumstances of his fateful and complex encounter he can be allowed an apparent misperception of other actions.

War is Seldom Fair

A few days later, I was flying as Flight Leader Canning's wingman in another four-plane flight. This time we found ourselves on the favorable end in a duel between superior and obsolete airplanes. We had been sent on a strafing mission, specifically to look for trains moving down the French and Italian coasts, destined for the front lines below Rome. Trains had pretty much quit running during daytime hours since our 52nd Group had arrived. As we approached the coastline near Cannes, Sully Burnett, called out, "Bogies on the deck, two o'clock low." As you may have guessed, "bogey" was the call name for unidentified aircraft. The call "bandit" was used as soon as any member of the formation identified the sighting as enemy aircraft.

The sighting turned out to be four observation planes, each towing a large glider. Apparently they were on a delivery to the Italian front. The Henschel HS – 126 was an obsolete machine used for all sorts of purposes.

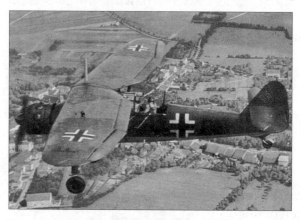

Henschel HS – 126
Photo courtesy of
www.warbirdsresourcegroup.org

These had a rear gunner with twin machine guns and some forward firing armament. Somebody shouted, "Bandits" when the black crosses on the 126s' wings flashed and Canning called "Tally Ho!" I followed him in a dive toward the lead plane and, as we approached, the 126s cut loose their gliders.

Canning's target was smart. He did what we had done against superior performance planes and made a tight turn into us just over the water. No way could one bend the gun sight toward the enemy's new direction. At Canning' order I turned after another 126 while he pursued the first escapee.

Although I was too busy to see them at this time, I could hear the chatter from Burnett and his wingman. It sounded clear, Burnett had knocked one of the enemy planes into the water. Momentarily, I lost sight of Canning. But I was boring in on my 126 and had slowed way down in an attempt to turn. It was almost the only way to line him up. The first time I got him briefly in the gun sight nothing happened when I pushed the firing button! In my excitement I had pushed the bomb release rather than the adjacent gun button! Tracers from the enemy gunner were flying all around my slow-moving Spit!

An Unlikely Loss

I continued to contort around him, barely missing the water. *Hey, damn it! ... quit that crap ... can't get a fudding bead!* Unexpectedly, he made a poor judgment with a turn and gave me a perfect target ... *Ahhhhhh you dumb bastard!!!* I raked him with machine gun fire and I could see I had hit the gunner. The 126 engine was ablaze. I broke off and watched the enemy plane nose into the sea.

I caught up with Canning who had splashed his first 126 into the sea and he was chasing the only remaining enemy plane. *Oh noooo!* A stream of white smoke was pouring from Canning's engine. This could mean only one thing, a coolant leak and an imminent engine failure. "Red one," I shouted, "You're losing coolant. Get some altitude quick!" As I neared, Canning pulled up sharply and shouted "May Day! God damn it!"

Out he went with his chute only just opening before he successfully landed in an open field. Apparently, a rear gunner hit his coolant line and he won a free pass to more than a year in a German prison camp.

I quickly targeted the guy Canning had been chasing. He led me into a town, between buildings in a virtual car chase. I was able to get in a couple of bursts at him.

In the meantime Burnett and his wingman had made sure that none of the gliders nor their contents were salvageable. Burnett cautioned about fuel levels and urged me to quickly join up at a predetermined spot and make for home. I had lost track of the re-

First Victory
Photo courtesy of Bob McCampbell

maining 126 due to his street smarts and a few low clouds. So, the hit-the-road call found a welcome ear. I did savor my first victory, as did Burnett. All the squadron guys were excited and made a big deal out of it because our bunch had faired so poorly in terms of knocking down enemy planes. Any aerial victory was a big deal. The loss of Canning was a dampener, but each of us was sometimes a little envious of such bad fortune. The selfish unspoken thought inevitably crept in that anyone taken prisoner without serious injury was relatively free from risking his butt any longer.

The other downer for me was the remorse I felt at the deaths, at my hands, of the enemy pilot and his gunner. By World War II, most aerial encounters were sufficiently distant and fleeting to avoid any intimate image of the terrible impact of their results. These encounters had been sufficiently slow and close up to allow me to witness the gunner's death and the apparent anguish of the disadvantaged 126 pilot.

We could bury our guilt in the depths of our military indoctrination, which characterized all enemy forces as inhuman fiends. The old standby "Its either them or me" worked pretty well. Still, I felt the emotion and sometimes still do. I realize these two were young men like my comrades and me ... others who undoubtedly would be deeply missed by loved ones. They were simply more of my generation who by virtue of the whimsies of war, would never be allowed the future that the roll of dice has given me to enjoy.

Riviera Revenge

We used to call Cannes harbor "Flak Alley". We could never understand what they were so avidly protecting. It seemed to us the Germans had more antiaircraft weapons concentrated in that small area than anywhere along the coast. Just around the bend, in the small picturesque harbor of Antibes, I had picked up a couple of flak holes while cruising by a bunker nestled in a sea cliff. The general word in the squadron was that unless you had been given a target in the Cannes/Antibes arena, it would be wise to cut a wide swath around that spot.

I thought that such a level of protection might be attributed to the German brass who enjoyed the place as an R&R, or rest and relaxation haven. A flight by some of our guys to Cannes had come upon the patio of a large bistro filled with German officers hoisting their hops. The flight just popped up off the water, spotted the soiree and swept the packed patio clean with gunfire.

Almost 40 years later my wife, Lois and I traveled to Antibes to visit our Canadian friends, Doug and Heather Campbell. On the first evening there, they invited us to have outdoor cocktails on their patio. We found ourselves lounging in deck chairs, on a concrete slab in the front of their rented home overlooking the calm, enchanting Antibes Bay. It turned out we were relaxing atop a leftover concrete German bunker ... one I could hardly forget. In early 1944, twin 20 mm cannon fire emanating from the bunker had surrounded my Spit with tracers so concentrated, I couldn't figure how they missed!

"Get No Promotion This Side of the Ocean"

In any combat zone during WWII it became an insult and a bit humiliating to have remained alive for as long as our bunch had and still be only a 2nd Lieutenant. You were viewed as someone just off the boat or a real screw up. Aside from the prestige factor, we lowest ranking officers were assigned the bottom of the barrel extra duty assignments, such as censoring mail, enlisted quarter's inspection, mess officer duty and other dull administrative chores. One of the duties I enjoyed least was that of overnight watch officer at the flight line. It was a lonely vigil ... no beer nor bullshit with my buddies. There were other undesirable aspects as well.

The duty watch officer's job was to spend the night in the ready room at the flight line about six miles from where the CO and most everybody else were relaxing. On actual guard duty over our airfield was a small contingent of French Moroccan soldiers headed up by a French officer. No one, including the officer, spoke English and some conversations ran their course without really communicating anything. The watch officer watched the phone and answered it, made a round or two of the airplanes, gas and bomb dumps and other facilities and could hit the sack for the night when he deemed it prudent.

On one occasion I answered a late night knock on the ready room door. I opened it to find myself face to face with a turbaned, bearded, Moroccan sergeant carrying a long ugly knife on his waist, a pistol in his holster and a rifle on his back. This formidable protector of our airbase gave me my first-ever, French salute and began speaking in perfect Moroccan. I knew it was perfect because it was perfectly unintelligible. Then he beckoned with his hand and pointed toward our maintenance hanger. Whew, what a relief! Finally a language I could understand ... gestureez.

As we approached the hanger I could see several of the other Moroccan soldiers standing around what appeared to be a somewhat roughed up young and frightened, Corsican civilian. Then up drove the French officer in charge of the Moroccan soldiers in his Jeep. This gathering culminated in an interrogation and an international conference among four monolinguals speaking French, Moroccan, English and Corsican (a blend of French and Italian). The good thing was that the French officer was somewhat fluent in Corsican and began sternly interrogating the suspect. I gathered that the youth (he looked like a teen) had been picked up walking a road along the periphery of our airfield. It occurred, that this was our military base and I didn't want to see the third degree, administered to some, perhaps, innocent Corsican kid without due process ... not on my watch.

I made a gesture like a phone call and scooted back to the ready room to call Sam Houston, my squadron CO. Sam was, as always, grumpy about having his sleep disturbed. Sam and his driver showed up in about 15 minutes and I was pleased to find he took the matter at hand more seriously than his sleep loss. Our stay in Calvi had brought us some sabotage attempts, albeit, rather inept ones. In our motor pool, just outside the Bonaparte Hotel, a grenade hidden under one of our truck hoods had detonated prematurely a fortnight before. Luckily, nothing but the truck was injured. It was the vehicle we boarded regularly as our personnel commuter between Calvi and the airfield. We also had discovered apparent attempts to doctor fuel tanks in a couple of the Spits, a matter of no minor concern to us pilots.

In the case of the captive Corsican kid, after days of grilling by the French and the local constabulary, the poor teen was absolved of evil intentions. I'm not sure if I was ever completely cleared of the crime of blowing reveille at midnight in CO Sam's ear.

Lusting for Duty

It was one of those watch worry evenings that Scofield, one of our middle-aged pilots, about twenty-five, offered to do me a favor. "Sco" proposed he serve my scheduled watch duty for me. "Sounds great to me, Sco ... but didn't you do watch duty just last night?" "Mac," He explains, "I've found a compatible friend who deeply shares my joy of watch duty." Now Sco, a tall lean charmer, certainly possessed all the fabled assets of a ladies' man. It followed that all of us to whom he had introduced his comely, compatible,

Corsican companion, agreed this was a match made in watch duty heaven.

They took up housekeeping in the ready shack during the cold winter nights, clearing out before the early morning squadron people arrived. It followed, that for a while, Sco all but eliminated our watch duty chore. Naturally, all of us were understandably disappointed when word inevitably leaked to the CO and Sco's watch duty monopoly was summarily scrapped. One must admit that Sco's tryst was an innovative one, considering the girl lived at home and Sco, like the rest of us, shared male-encumbered rooms.

What a Way to Go

During the first two weeks in March, 1944, about six of us were sent each day across the Island to a B–25 (Mitchell, medium bomber) base on the Corsican east coast. We were to join similar numbers from our 2nd and 5th Squadrons assigned to escort the B–25s on short interdiction bombing missions over Northern Italy. The Allied ground forces were still bogged down below Rome.

By this time I had become an element leader (a guy with a wing man) ... but still only a 2nd Lieutenant. No one ever got promoted in the 12th Air Force. Our new squadron CO, Trowbridge, was only newly promoted to captain. Anyhow, it happened to be my 21st birthday and I had already been greeted by people shooting at me. Not exactly a surprise party but after all I was now eligible to vote and drink. I was more eagerly anticipating the latter in celebrating the occasion. There was no question that I'd be celebrating mostly the fact that I had lived long enough to celebrate.

I'd flown one escort mission already that day and was thinking I could soon fly back to home base at Calvi, take a nap and go out on the town. Guess what? I was standing by my old faithful Spit, joking with a crew chief when Cummings, our flight leader yells down the line, "Hey Mac! We gotta make another milk run (slang for short easy mission). Let's grab a bite and go to the bomber briefing."

Not overly thrilled at this birthday bonus, I picked up McCauley by his plane along the way and slogged up to the bomber's mess hall. After the briefing we sat endlessly waiting for the slower bombers to get airborne and formed up. Typically for warriors of all sorts, war involves long periods of waiting and boredom contrasted with shorter periods of extreme focus, fear and fury.

Well, the last B–25 finally defied gravity and began gathering in formation. They circled the field and initiated an easterly heading toward northern Italy. The Spits then taxied out smartly, in predetermined order, taking off two at a time. My wingman, Goettleman, followed me closely. At the beginning of the runway we checked the instruments, the magnetos, mixture control, prop pitch and I gave a wave to Goettleman. He replied with a thumbs up and we started our roll down the rough dusty runway.

Spit Fit

Suddenly my plane began pulling uncontrollably to the left. Had my wingman not been tucked so tightly on my right I probably could have over-controlled to the right and gotten off the ground safely. With that in mind I chose to allow the plane to ease off onto the rough left side of the runway. With throttle to the wall and wheels folding I was bouncing and staggering into the air. Would have made it ... but, either a wing tip or the folding landing gear hit a bulldozed dirt pile bordering the runway. Bang! Bang! Crunch! Crumble! Thud! I was doing a dazzling, mid-air trapeze act and no outstretched arms in sight.

The Spit suddenly was cartwheeling, losing wings, scooting along upside down in the dirt and twisting, *"What a god awful way to go."* Ultimately, the thing wound up with nothing much left but a twisted cockpit, now almost removed from what formerly was a Spitfire. Although I never took time to flip off the switches, miraculously I escaped immolation and found I could run from the wreck. En route I ran across one of my discarded wings and sat down on it because my back was killing me.

A Mash Unit and No Martinis

At the local B–25 dispensary they put a bunch of stitches in my bleeding scalp. I had trouble walking so they tucked me into an ambulance with three wounded bomber crewmen from the previous mission ... destination, a M.A.S.H. unit. They then hauled me over some of the roughest roads I ever experienced. Each rut challenged by the ambulance stabbed me in the back. The other wounded were probably in more pain than I. Upon arrival at the M.A.S.H., no gurney for me and each step toward my assigned tent was agonizing. They did nothing for me at this place and I sensed they thought I was malingering.

After a few days McCauley and Tribbett flew back over to "Corsica East" for a visit. We went for a short walk and I was still in a lot of pain. Naturally, I took a lot of insults from these compassionate *compadres* like bucolic McCauley's, "Shat, Mac, can't you steer a fudding Spit down a runway?" They then went to talk to some of the top medics. Within a short time a M.A.S.H. Doc came to tell me I had been released to my squadron doctor.

Even though I was still hurting too much to walk very far, I was glad to be getting out of a hospital that seemed to be treating me only with suspicion. Naturally I queried my visiting buddies, "Why? After you guys, with absolutely no authority, talked to the medics ... you guys who know nothing about medicine except for the effects of medicinal alcohol on your dumb brains ... Why? Would the medics allow two such asses to spring me from here?" McCauley responding in pure Arkansan tongue replies, "Nothing to it Mac, Trib an me jus tole ole Colonel Cock Doc that they was right about y'all being a gold brick and a haperchonderwreck, and that we knew the Colonel needed the beds for guys what's really hurt."

With that they drove me by jeep to the base of the 5th Squadron in Bastia where the two had landed their planes. In about three more days I hooked a short hop on a C–47 (Military DC–3 airliner) back across Corsica to my Calvi. There our squadron, Doc Curran insisted on getting some back x-rays. The conclusions from these rather sketchy tests, while inconclusive, still seemed to be enough to have sent me stateside and out of harms' way. Also, I was experiencing sharp upper back pains with any kind of jarring movement. Yet, I was getting a little better day by day. I mulled over situation for a few days and reached a conclusion. I simply wasn't happy about leaning on my injury for a ticket home.

Perplexing Purple Heart

A few days later my Squadron CO, Captain Trowbridge and my Group CO Lieutenant Colonel Levine, called me in for a discussion that would ease my decision to stick it out. First Levine smiled and said, "Bob it's my honor to present you with the Purple Heart for wounds suf-

Purple Heart Head
Photo courtesy of Bob McCampbell

fered while fighting for your country." I reacted with an incredulous "Whaaaat?"

Levine and Trowbridge laughed and went on to explain that an investigating crew had found a sliver of antiaircraft shrapnel imbedded in the left tire of my Spit. Apparently I had picked it up over enemy territory along with some other underside dings while on the previous mission. The piece of flak had only gradually worked its way in and blown the tire as I was taking off on the second mission. I had been shot down by an enemy who will never have the satisfaction of knowing he did it. I had been neglectful in not better inspecting my horse between missions.

As he left I thanked and saluted the Colonel. Captain. Trow took over the conversation. "We're going to send you on leave Bob, along with a couple of the other guys who have so well earned it. The 12th Air Force has recently taken over several nice hotels on Capri. Because of your injury we've got special authority to allow you a two week stay there." I could only say, "Wow Trow!" He then added that if my injuries cleared up satisfactorily during my leave, he would be talking to me about possible added responsibilities.

Found Heaven Near Hell

Trib and I took a launch from Naples to Capri along with a bunch of other Air Force officers. Upon landing I didn't think I had ever seen a spot more picturesque. What heavenly serenity lying so near Armageddon. Trib and I shared a luxurious room in a five-star hotel on the top of the Island. Settling in between the clean white sheets the first night, seemed to be as good as it gets. I had been almost a year away from that sort of luxury.

The view from the windows throughout framed a panorama of Vesuvius, Sorrento, other magic islands and fishing boats rising out of that hypnotic azure sea. The dining room and bar were posh and surrounded by view windows. I thought we owned a Genie. Every service was available. A mesmerizing string quartet soothed the soul from breakfast to whenever. The only luxury lacking were beautiful women.

Capriciousness on Capri

Turned out, actually, there were attractive and surprisingly well-groomed young ladies to be found elsewhere on Capri. Seemed as though many Italian families of means had managed to find a haven from the war there and they had daughters. One evening we happened onto a dance being held in another of the incomparable Capri hotels. Trib and I ordered up and sat backward to the bar watching a rather classic, uptown ballroom dance scene. A fine Italian dance band enhanced the soiree and we couldn't help noticing several lovely well-dressed young women participating in the ritual. Only trouble was they all seemed to be taken.

Another fly boy whose name no longer filters through joined us at the bar. The three of us were particularly noticing a rather petite, dark haired, dark eyed, olive complexioned, beauty wearing a white sharkskin dinner dress and *"momma mia,* what a smile.*"* She was dancing with a young Navy Lieutenant who wasn't bad looking himself. As we paid a little more attention to him, all three of us realized there was something, somehow distinctly recognizable about the guy. Suddenly our new found fly boy friend stutters, "I – I, you know, it's the movie star, ah ... Preston, Robert Preston." Trib interrupts, "Yeah, that's who" and I added something like, "Guess that's him all right." (This was Robert Preston to be later famous for the song, *76 Trombones* and the long running lead on stage and screen in the *Music Man* musical.)

Our friend then insists one of us has got to cut in if we're going to get to dance with this girl. "Not me!" Says I. Trib turns to the bar and picks up three toothpicks, messes with them, palms them and orders, "Each of you guys take one and leave one for me. Short stick cuts in." Very reluctantly I drew one ... and you guessed it, I held the short stick. I thought about running out of the place, back to our hotel and hiding deep under my covers in the pre-natal position. It seemed a worse predicament than being shot at. I took a deep breath as I felt a solid push and reluctantly sauntered out on the dance floor. Then I, Robert nobody, tapped Robert Preston, movie star, on the shoulder. He politely acquiesced, and I found myself dancing and making sign language with Giovanna. She spoke little English. She had been sitting at a table with two other girls and eventually Trib and our bar-friend and I all wound up as a triple date.

The good news was that Giovanna and I somehow hit it off, even with the language barrier. The bad news was that another member of that lovely triad happened to be Giovanna's older sister. The sister was a cheerful, attractive girl as well, but failed to realize that in some situations three was a large crowd.

After a couple of days of enjoying chaperoned outings with Giovanna, I was even invited as a dinner guest to their rather enviable villa on Capri. Giovanna's father, who spoke some English and was obviously educated and articulate, owned a manufacturing plant in Milan. At this time the plant was in German occupied territory and I wondered how he could maintain much liaison with the business. Both he and the mother seemed to be sophisticated and pleasant sorts but for all I knew he could have been making munitions for the enemy.

Talk About Wartime Explosions

As preordained by squadron management, Trib went back to duty following our first week on Capri. With Giovanna for company, can't say I missed him terribly. I found her to be an all around beautiful person. We toured the Island together, even sometimes without chaperone. We visited the Roman baths and other caesarian antiquities and boated into the rapturous sequined waters of the Blue Grotto. Although the relationship by necessity had remained reasonably platonic, it still seemed heavy in this fairyland dream interrupting a war. Consequently, I had begun to have pangs of conscience about my sworn commitments far away back home.

Well, I guess the great old guy up there who had kept me alive thus far was trying to help me out of another of life's pitfalls. During the first days of my second week's stay, he suddenly interrupted the ambiance and staged one devilish diversion. He simply blew up Mount Vesuvius, in clear view, only about 15 miles across the waters on the Italian mainland. I had been walking down a walled stone path from my top of the island hotel toward Giovanna's villa when the earth shook and the volcano erupted.

Sounds like the consummation of a romance, doesn't it? Suppose it sort of was. My God, what a dazzling spectre ... and this was daytime! As night fell, I think I watched the most spectacular fireworks display ever. Cecil B. De Mille, eat your heart out! But soon the exploding debris and towering geysers of fire and lava were completely obscured by smoke and a blizzard of falling ash.

The accompanying quakes and eruptions continued for several days and falling rock wiped out more than half a B–25 light bomber group located near the base of the volcano. Some villages were destroyed. The worst thing for Capri was that it found itself almost knee deep in ash. For several days, the gray soot continued to fall and anyone venturing outside, quickly looked like a gray zombie. Hair and mustaches were particularly vulnerable.

Ciao Capri

As one might imagine, life on the beautiful Isle had become a bit disrupted with the mess ... including my romance. Providentially, the day before my destined departure it rained on Capri, Vesuvius took a slumber and the Isle, inevitably sparkled again. The night before my returning to the squadron, Giovanna and I went dancing at the hotel where we'd met. Her ever-watchful sister was there too, which was probably another blessing for us both. The following day Giovanna gave me a big hug and a teary kiss as I boarded the launch. She also handed me an oil painting she had done of the fishing boats resting on the small harbor beach at Capri ... *a la* Van Gogh's. It was a happy painting. It was April of 1944. It was not a happy moment.

Chapter 10

Mustang Rules the Range

New Steeds, New War

For a month or so a big change had been brewing for the three squadrons of the 52nd Fighter Group. We were going to be outfitted with the vaunted North American P–51B Mustang. We were to be transferred to the 15th Air Force for long range bomber escort. Many of the fighter outfits in England had received Mustangs in late 1943. As I mentioned earlier, they had certainly lived up to their advance billing. Not only was their range unique among the world's fighters, but the 51 could outperform anything else. Being just an average fighter pilot myself, the 51 sounded like my kind of plane.

We had heard a certainly positive address from a visiting 8th Air Force pilot with combat experience in 51s. We had studied the Mustang flight manuals and time was approaching to say, "Hello Mustangs" and "Farewell faithful Spits." The CO (Trowbridge) and Tim Tyler, our then senior flight leader, had flown to Algiers and picked up the first two of our 51s.

I'd hardly got a chance to look them over when Trow says, "Mac need you and Bullock, Grew and Montgomery to pick up four more 51s tomorrow. You feeling OK, Mac?" "Fine." I answered. I had told Doc Curran the same thing. Actually, both my upper and lower vertebrae still were painful in activities such as the jar from the routine exit jump off my plane wing.

Trow says, "Mac you're in charge and pick up the paperwork in the adjutant's office."

Fly or Flinch Time Again

A C–47 picked us up about 0900 for a long lumbering flight of about 600 miles to Algiers on the North African coast. My God! How luxurious. When we picked up Spits we hitch-hiked half way across North Africa to the British depot. This time we landed at a vast American air depot, storing numbers of every plane flown by the Army Air Forces. We eventually found our way to a large two-story building facing out over the endless array of airplanes. An army captain met me and my papers from behind a long, high counter. He obviously wondered what a scruffy 2nd lieutenant was doing in charge of anything.

I wondered why I wasn't a captain like this guy, hundreds of miles from harm's way. I would probably bed down at night in my own "Med-vista" room, between clean sheets ... and have a line-up of beautiful gals outside my door vying for the privilege of sharing my accommodations.

At any rate the captain had me sign more papers and then pointed saying, "Lieutenant, about a quarter of a mile out you can see some 51s just before you get to those 17s. The corporal standing outside by the jeep will take you and your gear out there where you'll find the P–51 crew chief waiting. He'll help you check out. The driver will bring your other pilots on his next trip." The captain suggested that since none of us had checked out in the 51, it would be advisable for me to check out first as the more experienced of the group and then brief the others. I wasn't sure I agreed with his analysis of my superior experience, but whatever we did in checking out I hoped none of us screwed up while doing it.

North American P – 51B
Photo courtesy of U.S. Air Force

Introduction to a Mustang

The tech sergeant with the 51s did an excellent job of giving me a stem to stern review of the airplane and its technicalities. None the less I was a bit surprised that no pilot was around to go over flight characteristics, instrument settings and control idiosyncrasies. I've got to admit I was a bit apprehensive, as I'm sure the others were ... or would be, concerning an imminent maiden voyage in this or any fighter.

The others had arrived for their briefing by the crew chief as I was strapping myself into my new home. I started up, waved to the guys and taxied out through a maze of land-locked military planes. I carefully went through the checklist; prop in low-pitch, mixture control rich, fuel levels and shoved the throttle steadily toward the wall.

With the smooth purr of the Rolls Royce driving the big four-bladed prop, the craft quickly grabbed the air and thrust us forward. Due to its widely spaced landing gear it was much easier than the Spit to control on take-off.

As I lifted off and climbed to a couple of thousand feet I noticed a more effortless control and about a 50 mph higher cruising speed than the Spit V.

On this first outing I merely took the Mustang for a couple of whirls around the airport. Returning, I was lucky enough to grease-in an almost perfect three point landing near the beginning of the runway. What a time to do it while the other guys were watching so closely. Taxiing in, the crowd of three pilots and one tech sergeant gave a big, thumbs-up. All the wonderfully positive stuff I had felt about my short flight in the airplane I immediately shared with the guys. But partly as a legitimate caution and partly to blow my own leadership horn, I reminded the others that the 51 touches down about 20 mph faster than the Spit and that on the very short Calvi runways they better drop the birds within the first hundred feet.

Well, Bullock, Grew, and Montgomery each successfully soloed his 51 and came back with the same euphoric praise for the airplane. We decided we would each take another flight, this time up at altitude, to wring the 51s out (do some aerobatics) and get a better feel for the plane. This experience made everyone even more thrilled with the 51's performance and handling. With that I led the flight back to Calvi, Corsica in about half the flying time to do the trip in the C–47. Two of the guys had to take extra tries to squeeze the 51s onto the Calvi airstrip. Trowbridge was happy to see us ... and his four additional Mustangs, safe and sound in their new home.

Tenting Tonight

A few more trips to Algiers by other squadron pilots and we had filled our complement of about twenty P–51B Mustangs. As a full squadron of new airplanes and some replacement pilots we made a few more training flights out of Calvi. I was made a flight leader and we were soon moved in mid-April to the eastern side of Corsica. We did inherit a longer runway there. None too soon, I guessed. We had been having some close calls with those meager Calvi pasture runways. We were back into three pilots to a tent living accommodations. The country-side was green, rolling, bushy and kind of reminded me of the Ojai, California foothill area. Cattle and other livestock grazed hither and yon. Gratefully, we accepted the warming spring temperatures of the "Med" climate. It had been a cold winter in Calvi even with indoor living.

Spies Demise

I can't remember any good reason why, but, one day in April, 1944, McCauley and I revisited Calvi. We each took a Mustang back over to our old airstrip. We hitched a ride into town and said hello to some friends left behind. One was the priest at the small church in midtown. This is where several of us pilots had thrown a 1943 Christmas party for the parish kids. We had, at the time, collected at least 50 pounds of "Life Saver" rations sent to our squadron from the U.S. These served as tree decorations. The ecstatic Calvi kids, led by the padre, had responded with Christmas carols in French, and especially for us, a rendering of *Home On The Range* in broken English. Their infectious joy at the treats and touching song offerings were a moving holiday reward for all of us.

We also paid a visit to a shop-keeper, who had helped with the kids' party, a favorite bartender, and our old buddy, Reggie, the captain of the British rescue patrol boat. He, of course, insisted we drop on board and revisit the "Sparklets" water bottle's bottomless supply of vermouth. Finally, at the harbor we ran into the grizzled, bearded, old French schooner captain who smuggled arms and cutthroats in and out of the mainland for the French underground. His name escapes me, but understandably he'd had an envious wealth of intriguing tales to tell. He had one yet to finish involving McCauley and me. When we heard the conclusion of that one, I wished we hadn't asked. To put all this into some perspective, D-Day and the liberation of France were still months away

So, looking back at the Calvi of mid-February, 1944, it had been a time of continuing day to day combat missions in our tired old Spitfires. We had discovered a downtown Calvi bar that was smartly appointed and surprisingly well-stocked. Here we found surprisingly tasty knackwurst and other deli sandwiches as well as a full-ranging drink menu. A few of us began substituting this bill of fare for our evening army mess menu. It beat wartime restaurant food in the States. Where did they find such gourmet food?

The bar was owned and run by a handsome, smartly groomed, well-educated and polished husband and wife in their fifties. They spoke in proper King's English with a slight German accent. The couple advised they were Dutch expatriates. No question, we wholly enjoyed their conversation. I felt I was in the presence of a lord and lady of an English manor ... not that I had ever experienced such social interaction. One evening McCauley and I were enjoying some of this repartee` with "Lord of the bar" and a drink when there occurred a noticeable shift in the conversation. His lordship gradually got into questions that seemed definitely inappropriate, such as " ... well chaps, what sort of exciting things did you find today" and "what do you fellows think will be up for tomorrow?"

Early on in the questionable questions, McCauley had cast me a side-glance and I'd returned it with a raised eyebrow. McCauley, answers with something like, "Dammed if me and Mac didn't find a couple of Calvi cuties just lookin' for fun down by the harbor this afternoon." I interrupted, adding, "Yeh, and McCauley's definition of fun never seemed to be the same as theirs, ha ha." Our trying to be funny with responses to a few more such questions appeared to be falling flat and we began changing the subject. Eventually, we excused ourselves and headed for the CO's lair at the Bonaparte Hotel. Strangely, the captain didn't get too worked up over our barroom tale and advised he'd have someone look into the situation. We left feeling that our boss had just condescendingly brushed off some spy revelations from the Hardy Boys.

After days of agonizing over whether or not we were dealing with a real or imagined spy problem, we masterminded a plan ... a sort of a sting, if you will. It eludes me whose idea it was but McCauley and I decided to pay a visit to the bar in question while feigning a slight overdose of spirits. It had to be done at the right moment. When that finally came, it was late in the evening and fortunately we were the only customers. We sat at a table and ordered a drink from the bar while loudly reveling in each other's attempts at humor. I think I had proclaimed that It was my birthday. Our Dutch host bought drinks on the house and ask if he and his wife might join us. We were overjoyed.

The conversation meandered around a seemingly genuine interest in McCauley's and my separate lives growing up in America, our parents lives and the towns we lived in. We responded with similar wishes to learn about their personal lives and interests. Eventually and predictably, the war became the focal topic and our hostess brought us another round. As we sort of anticipated, it took no time for a narrower focus to subtly zoom in on our own little part of the war. "How long can your Spitfires stay up when you are carrying bombs?" "Where does your petrol come from?" "How many fellow pilots have you lost since you have been here?" "What places in Southern France are the best places to target. "What sort of place will you be flying to tomorrow?"

These kinds of questions were separated by our hosts' rather innocuous small talk about their con-

cerns about us or perhaps hopes for our safe early return home. But they kept coming and McCauley and I
kept dodging answers, often by drunken sounding hi-
larity. Finally I stood and thanked the Lord and Lady
for their hospitality and told McCauley I was helping
him home while I still could.

Now before the squadron had moved from Calvi
we'd had the opportunity of asking the French schooner captain if he knew anything about the Lord and
Lady bar keepers. He did know of them and the bar.
We then told him about our barroom interrogations
"*Ah oui,* I know of other problems zat zey have. We
muse veezeet zat seetuaysiohne, tut suit"

On our return visit to Calvi in April, we had
found the Lord and Lady's bar boarded shut. When
we found the French underground captain in port we
couldn't wait to ask if he knew what had happened
with the bar keeper couple. "*Ah oui, mon ami.* Zey wair
German spies ... Zer was no quaysteeohne ... Zey wair
shot". Earlier on, I had been unsettled with our CO's
brush off of our suspicions. Now I felt far worse to find
our words had been acted upon so summarily.

Bull vs Mustang or Home on the Range

We move forward again with our saga and rejoin life at our new base on the eastern side of Corsica.
We did a little hiking around the area and found a
nice stream and pool big enough for bathing which
was always welcome ... but cold! From mid April on
until I was returned to the States in September, 1944,
personal hygiene was mostly maintained by a wash
cloth dipped into water heated in a GI helmet over a
Coleman stove.

Back to operations, although the runway was
composed of sheets of interlocking steel matting, the
ground it was laid on kicked up a lot of dust during take-offs. One morning as I was readying a take
off on a training flight, the dust from the flight tak-

ing off ahead of me suddenly looked like a tornado. Then I realized there had been an accident. It seems three cows had wandered across the runway obscured by dust and *ole*, had been speared by two Mustangs! The cows all suffered terminal wounds but so had two Mustangs. Remarkably, neither pilot had been injured and two speedy and enterprising mess cooks arrived and butchered the beasts before the dust had cleared. Our entire squadron relished rare beefsteak dinners from the improbable Mustang round up.

Back to Business

The 4th of May we flew our first heavy bomber escort mission. But it didn't turn out to be business as usual. Yes, we were again flying fighters over enemy territory and getting shot at each time we did, but business was quite different. First big change, naturally was the Mustang itself. Second thing was the inevitable sore butt from the long duration of the heavy bomber raids. Third difference was the ever increasing size of the raids in terms of numbers of bombers as well as numbers of escorting fighters. We're talking about maximum efforts of more than five hundred heavies and maybe a hundred fighters on one mission. A far cry from the two to four plane nuisance sorties our squadron of Spitfires had been flying out of Calvi.

Other business had changed as well. In mid May, 1944, the three squadrons of the 52nd Fighter Group, the 2nd, the 5th and ours the 4th, had been relocated onto a single base in a southern Italian wheat field along side the Adriatic Sea. We were again a tent city. Our squadron, however did quickly build its own Officers Club ... well, mess hall and bar. The guys of the other squadrons were well dispersed from our area and we saw little of them on a social basis. However, we were all corralled for pre-mission briefings each morning at our 52nd Group headquarters building. Likewise we gathered together for post mission debriefing.

Certainly there were many other aspects of the long-range escort business to learn, especially as a flight leader. Many were gleaned through on the job training. Many were learned through postmortem seminars around the bar. In the interest of avoiding boredom I will mention only a few of the more critical.

First, management of fuel consumption was paramount. The average escort flight lasted over five hours, a few well over six. We zig-zagged over the bombers since they were a lot slower but we still wound up 500 or 600 miles from our base as we covered them to the target. The 51 was burning, on average, about a gallon per minute on cruise settings and that it was a long way to walk to the nearest gas station. The internal fuel tanks consisted of a tank within each wing holding 92 U.S. gallons apiece and a fuselage tank behind the pilot with 85 gallons. As a bonus we carried two 75-gallon drop tanks under the wings. We carried well over 400 gallons of 130-octane gas on takeoff.

Just Fueling Around

There were so many variables involved and guesses needed in fuel planning that in retrospect I don't know how most of us fared as well as we did. You could estimate the average gallon-per-minute consumption at particular rpm, but who could predict what the operational situations would demand or for what durations. Throttle settings under combat conditions gobbled gas fast.

Fortunately there were fuel gauges for the internal tanks which could advise how you were doing versus estimated distance home, but none for the drop tanks. These had to be gauged by noting time in use on your wrist watch. Perhaps the biggest variable was created by the unknown point at which you might be forced to jettison the drop tanks. Ideally, we would be lucky enough to hold on to our drop tanks till we ran the things dry.

As you've no doubt guessed the drop tanks had to go whenever combat action appeared imminent. Their additional weight and wind resistance severely limited combat performance. So, obviously the thing to do was to use the drop tanks fuel first ... Well, not quite. The fuselage tank when full made the plane tail heavy and clumsy. Rule one had to be modified.

Each pilot tended to tailor the fuel usage guidelines to fulfill his own perceived needs to maintain a proper feel of his airplane. But typically, we taxied out and took off on the fuselage tank. It was especially tough forming up with that full tank challenging the pilot for control. When half the fuel was burned from the fuselage tank, you switched to the left drop tank.

To maintain balance, each drop tank was tapped alternately for about 10-minute intervals. Finally each drop tank was run dry, that is if the enemy didn't force you to drop them earlier. If the latter happened, a switch was immediately made to one of the main internal wing tanks while simultaneously releasing the drop tanks. The main tanks were tapped alternately to maintain weight balance and flight stability.

Fuels Rush Out

Of course to maximize fuel availability, each tank was eventually emptied saving all remaining fuel, or say the last fifteen minutes worth, in one internal tank. A fleeting shock apparently common to us all was the inevitable interrupted heartbeat each time a tank ran dry and the engine inevitably coughed and quit. You never seemed to be ready for that experience as often as it happened. Fortunately the 51s almost always restarted easily.

On the homeward-bound trip we would regularly climb to around 30,000 feet and lean the fuel mixture to the point where the engine would minimally churn but was optimally fuel-efficient. Generally, the Luftwaffe attacked the bombers on the way in to the target or for only short distances on the return. We still could see a lot of sky from that altitude and maintain adequate vigil over our bombers. On occasion, a few of our group's guys did come up short on gas. Some simply didn't make it back. Some landed on the Italian beaches or alternate airstrips.

On a mid-day, coming back from a long mission, one of our guys had landed just behind me and had rolled to a stop in the middle of the runway. This turned out to be my old buddy, Pappy Gross. I had parked and caught a jeep over to where ground crew were feverishly pulling the plane off the runway. Pap had run dry just as he touched down without enough gas to taxi off. I shouted, "Christ, Pappy. You own this air strip or something?" "Mac" He says, "Can you believe anybody else can manage gas on a six hour, thousand mile run to come out this perfect?"

"Pappy!" McCauley interrupts, coming up from behind. "A good pilot would'a shut the fudder down on the way in, dead-sticked the SOB and saved enough hundred and thirty octane to clean his shorts!"

American Horn of Plenty

What a difference between the little war we fought out of Corsica and this one. U.S. production of both planes and pilots was spilling over and on top of the Axis nations. Only in retrospect have I appreciated the miraculous metamorphosis of our nation. We had darted from a third rate military power in 1942 to the position of world's most powerful nation by 1944. Implausibly, it had all happened during my short span of military service. I had been a minute product of this brilliant effort. My early-on impatience with the understandable mistakes of our unprepared nation as it was thrust into war overnight, now seems embarrassingly *naïve*. Strangely, I had been too wrapped up in my own new work and worries to fully grasp the historic magnitude of this incredible, once in a forever, accomplishment.

So here we were, assembled with thousands of bombers and fighters and trained flyers poised to venture forth through enemy skies. There is little doubt that each of us recognized our responsibilities to each other, to a great nation and to a world in peril. But now in our new combat role, we were beginning to focus more on honing our skills toward the success and welfare of the bombers and their crews.

My Position Description

I had flown 30 operational sorties and 40 combat missions in Spitfires, mainly as a wingman and later as an element leader.

From May 1944, until being sent home in early September, I would complete 41 additional combat missions in Mustangs. These were predominately long range escort missions and all in a leadership role. Sometime in May, Trowbridge had been returned to the states. Capt. Tim Tyler, a well-liked and certainly capable commanding officer, had replaced Trow as our new CO. No one could help but admire Tim's cool organized leadership in combat. During that late spring and ensuing summer, Tim personally accounted for eight aerial victories over enemy fighters.

Due to attrition during our previous small war, Tribbett, Bullock, McCauley, Gross and I had become senior in the squadron, but not by rank. We were all still 2nd lieutenants. Tribbett and I hit it off with Tyler surprisingly well considering that Trib was the silent type and I was not exactly swashbuckling. Tyler resubmitted promotions for all five of us and assigned Tribbett as operations officer and me as senior flight leader. This made Trib second in command and me sort of third. A degree of personality clash between Jim McCauley and Tyler allowed Jim to move into a group headquarters operations job.

Now, while this might not sound like much, it turned out to be a lot more than just a fancy title for me. Tim couldn't fly all of the missions what with administrative duties including commanding maybe 35 officers and about 200 men. Also, he was not expected to fly without a few days off here and there. Secondly, Trib, who would normally be scheduled to fly as squadron leader when the CO wasn't, contracted a chronic ear infection which occasionally grounded him. I wound up during that summer, leading the squadron on 15 missions and leading the entire fighter group on three of those. Finally, in July I was promoted to 1st Lieutenant.

My missions ran the gamut from tenuous to tiring, and from tedious to, terrifying. We could always count on plenty of high altitude anti-aircraft and its insidious black blooming sky bouquets, welcoming us to major European cities and industrial complexes. These pyrotechnics, along with a myriad of other cockpit requirements, were enough to keep me constantly on alert, even without air-to-air combat engagements. Perhaps any attempt to accurately resurrect youthful emotions, especially in that now-remote wartime environment, is a mission impossible. But, I can, with confidence, summarize that a welcome change in my emotional orientation in the combat atmosphere was clearly underway. I know that if the word terrifying connoted there were situations wherein my fears were seriously disabling, such would not be correct. Clearly, something was rewriting a few pages of my psychological makeup more in the direction of an ability to react to fear with positive actions.

Our fighter hierarchy had a policy that demanded we stay close to our bombers and not engage the enemy unless our bombers were attacked. Each fighter group was assigned specific bomber groups to protect and for the most part we stayed with them. This meant that on many missions we flew for considerable distances with enemy squadrons almost escorting us ... out of range, but not attacking. The enemy was clearly searching for an unprotected group of heavies, a friendlier atmosphere where, for one reason or another, Allied fighter protection was absent.

We, as well as our comrades in the other two squadrons, champed at the bit each time this enemy escort occurred. And it was frequent. This "let'em-be policy" was a questionable one among us and, as I later learned, at higher command levels as well. I have to admit that our 52nd Group was awarded a Distinguished Unit Citation for losing no bombers to enemy fighters on a June 9, 1944 mission. This involved providing escort on a massive heavy bomber assault against aircraft plants and supporting industry in the Munich, Germany region. The stick-with-the-bomber policy was maintained on this sizable mission.

We learned later, that the 8th Air Force (flying out of England) had modified that policy in early summer 1944. The 180° change encouraged seeking out the enemy, thus emphasizing the objective of saving the bombers by destroying the Luftwaffe.

No question, the Luftwaffe did eventually fritter away during late 1944 and continued to decline until the German surrender in May 1945. But this happened only after it was hit with overwhelming air superiority, attrition of experienced pilots, loss of production capabilities and fuel shortages. On the other hand, our bombers left without escort for one reason or another continued to suffer more serious losses than those which enjoyed close support. The old policy may have been a good one at a time when the opposing air powers were more balanced. After all, close support did get an acceptable force of bombers through to their targets ... something that wasn't happening until a significant force of long range P–51 escorts were employed. Going after enemy fighters in the air and on the ground in hot pursuit may have sacrificed some bombers, but more quickly eliminated the opposition. You may recognize, as these memoirs play out, we didn't exactly always stick to the dogma.

Fighter Pilot Who Couldn't Shoot Straight?

I was a lousy shot. I did fine at other aspects of being a fighter pilot, including some successful aerial leadership roles. Forming up the squadron; maintaining it in proper formation, altitude and deployment under varied conditions; navigation and managing timely rendezvous with assigned bombers and airmanship in general were things I felt pretty satisfied with.

Still I couldn't exactly shoot straight. Aerial gunnery was a skill best accomplished by skeet shooters or duck hunters. It just seemed that all the airplanes that I tried to shoot down weren't very cooperative and obviously were more interested in converting me into the "shootee" rather than my preferred role as the "shooter."

A Munich Eunuch

On June 9, 1944, the date of the unit citation, I remember we were flying at about 28,000 feet as top cover for B–24 bombers. We were, as always, weaving back and forth for better coverage and to avoid outdistancing our herd. The best I can recall, the mission was targeting aircraft assembly plants on the outskirts of Munich, Germany. I was leading Tackle Blue Flight and Tyler was leading the squadron. Clearing the higher Italian Alps and about 50 miles out from the bomber target we spotted three ME–109s, only about a mile ahead and slightly above us. They suddenly rolled over and dove vertically, wide open, at our bombers.

"Tackle Blue, Red One here," shouts Tyler, "Your Bandits! Get em!"

I called out "Tally Ho!" as I rolled on my back, followed by Bullock and our two wing men. We all pulled the 51s through into vertical pursuit. Our three adversaries with too great a head start were headed straight through the bomber formation. The 51 could build up such speed in a power on, vertical dive that as it neared the speed of sound you could experience severe buffeting and loss of control. You could also experience loss of a wing in attempting too sharp a pullout at such speeds. Normally, a Mustang could overtake a 109 in any kind of a down hill sprint but these guys were wide open with a good head start.

Messerschmitt ME - 109
Photo courtesy of
www.warbirdsresourcegroup.org

While Bullock and I were gaining on the 109s, we were both way over the air speed indicator "red line". We both were suffering control problems as we chased the wild enemy pilots right through the bomber formation. The 109s never had a chance to accurately fire at the bombers as they tore through at such unmanageable vertical speeds.

But there must have been a bunch of shaken bomber crews as the 109s tailed by Mustangs, all in screaming dives, somehow avoided collisions with a tightly packed flock of B–24s. Talk about shaken. Our marginally controlled sifting through that mass of heavies still gives me nightmares. It was another example in my military flying where luck replaced inadequate skills.

The enemy fighters split three directions. I tagged on to one and Bullock chased another. Our wingmen had lost us in the initial high-speed dive. Couldn't really blame them under the circumstances. Bullock and I had managed to squeeze off a couple of short bursts as our quarries dove. Neither of us saw any hits as we lost them in a ground haze.

Tyler had guessed right sending only one flight after the culprits. These 109s had been sent as decoys to draw off at least one of our squadrons while a larger enemy force attacked the bombers. Tyler and the rest of our squadron, along with the 2nd and the 5th squadrons, had tangled with the larger force, scored several victories and chased them off. Bullock and I were able to rejoin one another but couldn't relocate our squadron.

Typically, after a "do" such as this our guys had become pretty well scattered. Bullock and I had struggled back up to bomber altitude, and found some heavys returning without "Little Friends" as they called us. We covered these B–24s and got them home safely, but not with the guys what brought them. Fortunately, our wingmen had made it back as well. Bullock and I had made it home but empty handed. After reading the War Department Citation we rationalized that our chase contributed to our bombers' completing their mission without loss to enemy fighters.

Foiled Again?

A few days later we were back on the road to Munich with another herd of B–24s. Tim had mentioned at chow the night before that I would be leading the squadron. Normally I only learned of this last minute, substitute honor after breakfast. But then, I really preferred to hear such news in the morning because the previous night's sleep went better. As usual it was still dark through the briefing by Lt. Col. Levine and as we jeeped out to the airstrip for start up. The dawn was breaking as I raised my arm high out of my canopy, and waved the standard circular motion signaling, *start engines.*

We took off in twos with each wing man tucked in tight along the narrow runway. A green flare was lofted as a take off signal to each squadron. It was the 5th Squadron's turn to lead so their leader, Capt. Bob Curtis, had led them off first. He started his wide circle above the airstrip to allow each succeeding squadron to play catch-up by narrowing the circle. After all, we had to assemble as many as 48 fighters to head out on course at a specific time. I use the term "as many as" because 16 fighters per squadron was always the complement goal. Maintenance couldn't always field that many and a few would have to turn back after encountering engine or other mechanical malfunctions.

We all experienced a rough engine syndrome from time to time. If you concentrated hard enough you could hear all sorts of mysterious noises going on in that big 12 cylinder Rolls Royce engine. Pilots occasionally requested an early return to the dismay of a squadron leader ... but also to the bedevilment of the poor crew chief who couldn't hear the same rough engine sounds or locate a mechanical problem. Of course real mechanical problems did occur. Fortunately for me, none ever turned me back, but often, as the redoubtable Rolls droned ever on I heard questionable pops, squeaks and hums.

On our second Munich adventure, we rendezvoused with the bombers on time, just as they reached the Italian Alps. Our three 52nd Group Squadrons had begun our weaving over the B–24s and, as ever-necessary craning our necks, for enemy fighters. Our squadron was flying medium cover with the 2ⁿᵈ Squadron top cover at about 26,000 feet, us at 24,000 and the 5ᵗʰ Squadron, low cover at about 22,000. The bombers' formations were plodding along at about 21,000 feet. Although I can't remember the exact numbers, there were typically 500 B–17s and B–24s strung out from 50 to 75 miles. There were also four or five fighter groups, each responsible for one hundred or so bombers.

As we neared the same area of the previous Munich mission, the bombers began their turn for the bomb run and ... *Oh boy! Been here before!*

"Tackle Red, Bandits at 3 o'clock high!" called Swede Larson, leading yellow flight, just to my starboard.

"Yellow one, on 'em, they're goin diving, Get 'em Swede!"

This time it was two Focke-Wulf 190s diving toward the bombers and as Tyler had done before, I sent a flight after the decoys. We could all hear the chatter as Swede's flight tangled with the 190s. "Got you! You SOB!" came the welcome cry from Swede.

Only glitch in this *déjà vue* bit was the outcome. On the last trip, Tyler had subsequently run

Focke-Wulf – 190
Photo courtesy of
www.warbirdsresourcegroup.org.

into the main force of enemy fighters and added to his victories. All I got was a loge earphone seat listening to the pilots of the 31st Group engaging an obviously numerous enemy force. This force decoyed us but for some reason concentrated on the bomber group covered by the 31st, about 20 miles behind us.

Though it was a common experience on missions, none of us ever got hardened to the grievous spectacle of the loss of our bombers as they were hit by anti-aircraft fire over the heavily defended targets. Munich was defended by several hundred radar-controlled, heavy anti-aircraft weapons. It wasn't uncommon to see five or six heavies go down over the target area and others fall off along the return skyway. A deep felt prayer was always aroused that each crew member would safely extricate himself. We silently pleaded for the sight of ten parachutes safely blossoming from each fatally wounded bomber.

I had led the squadron past this typical mission scene and was resuming escort position for the trip home. Swede and I had communicated and I had found him and his flight using precious fuel to regain altitude to rejoin us. I had advised Curtis, the group leader, "Clatter Red One from Tackle Red One. Making wide 180 to reform Tackle Yellow Flight."

Curtis answered, "Roger Tackle Red,"

Swede did a victory roll as he came in sight and his flight formed up with us as we completed our circle. I was sure happy to see Swede ... even if I was a bit jealous.

Foiled by the Future

As I was increasing air speed to get the squadron back in originally assigned escort position, I spotted what appeared to be a lone twin-engine fighter ahead and about 2,000 feet above us. A wild hair got me, I turned the squadron over to Swede, and with my wing man, Bofinger, took after the bogey. I knew that at 25,000 feet a Mustang could catch any fighter the Germans had. I was wide open and closing on what looked to be an easy prey, if I could just identify the strange thing. I armed my guns and got close enough so I was sure he had German insignia.

It was at this moment he must have seen me. He poured the juice to the thing. I could no longer gain on him and he soon left me hanging out to dry. My wing-man, Bofinger, transmitted, "Red one! It's a jet!"

The realization had hit me by then that this was a Messerschmitt 262 jet fighter; a thing we had been briefed about but had never seen by mid-year 1944. I later learned they were using the few jets available for reconnaissance or for running down our own "recco" planes.

"Eyes to the skies, Bo, that thing could come back and bite." But he didn't.

The ME–262 turned out to be an amazingly advanced airplane for its time. Adolph Hitler had tried to convert it to a bomber and had thereby seriously delayed its desperately needed introduction as a fighter in any substantial numbers. In early 1945, well after I had left the European Theater, the Germans were able to mount fighter versions in formidable numbers. I recall reading that on one intercept they lofted more

Messerschmitt ME - 262 Jet
Photo courtesy of
www.warbirdsresourcegroup.org

than thirty ME 262 jet fighters The effect was serious and an unacceptable number of bombers were lost.

Luckily, the advent of the ME–262 was too late to make a difference in the outcome of the war. I should also mention that a few of the 262s were shot down by American P–51 pilots, often in situations where the U.S. pilots caught the 262s landing or taking off. There were also a few victories scored by P–51 pilots where their inexperienced 262 adversaries slowed to mix it with 51s and were out maneuvered. Unfortunately, I was not one of these 51 pilots.

Me, a Safe Haven for the Luftwaffe?

Near as I can gather from my vague and tattered records, it was on 22 June '44 and Tyler was leading the squadron. This time we were escorting B–17s targeting aircraft works near Vienna, Austria. I was leading Tackle Yellow Flight with Bullock and Grewe making up my other element and I had a new wingman. I'll call him Burns since for reasons rather sad I prefer not to use his real name.

Burns was a likable, naïve 19-year-old from a prominent oil family, who only days earlier had been assigned to the squadron (I was a sophisticated 21 year old), so I had taken him under my wing for training in our provincial squadron ways. He, with his family's help I'm sure, had managed to find some string puller to fulfill his ultimate wish to become a fighter pilot. He "couldn't wait to shoot down an enemy plane" (I wanted to tell him, "Me neither.")

Burns was a good kid but awfully eager. In his brief time since flying school he had been assigned to Air Transport Command flying C–47s. During our training sessions he had certainly shown ability to manage the Mustang and fly formation. But he seemed to unnecessarily gyrate around my tail like a puppy as he followed me through maneuvers.

Burns had been a champion Golden Gloves boxer. Jim McCauley, who was about Burns' size and fancied himself a good amateur, had taken him on with gloves for a little sparring outside the tents one day. I think Jim decided in a hurry that stopping after one short round was prudent. In a later situation one of the pilots wound up in a sort of hazing engagement with Burns which culminated in a pie-like something landing in Burns' face. A challenge ensued resulting in a boxing match. Although the tormentor clearly out-weighed Burns, the guy was outclassed in the match to the point of double pay back humiliation. Burns could have killed him.

On our Vienna mission, we were covering the tail-end-charlies of the heavy bomber raid and we began to hear some wild chatter from squadrons ahead. Apparently, they had run into some heavy and unusual air opposition. ME–109s and FW–190s were covering twin engine ME–110 fighters attempting to broadside

Messerschmitt ME – Bf 110
Photo courtesy of
www.warbirdsresourcegroup.org

the bombers with rockets. There had been a melee that we were rapidly approaching.

Tim was alerting us about some 109s he was pursuing but the airwaves were so overloaded with a deafening static of calls, I couldn't read the rest of his words. The fear and excitement were peaking. Two 110s that had spent their rockets suddenly swept by us and were attempting to dive by and away. I closed in on one, Bullock and his wingman chose another. We were both firing at the separate 110s. But in split seconds we were overshooting our slower targets. I saw strikes on my quarry, stitching and spanning each black crossed wing and did a knee-jerk dodge to avoid a collision. As I yanked the stick around into a tight turn to try again, I realized my wingman, Burns, was gone.

It was simultaneously evident that the 110 was still struggling down and away on one engine. I quickly went back alone to finish off my wounded 110. I slowed this time, was working him into my gun sight and ... My God No! ... tracers were screaming by my port side. I chopped the throttle, jammed the stick forward and prayed. A diving FW–190 overran me so close I could touch him. The enemy pilot, providentially, had been a kindred spirit who couldn't shoot straight either. As I maneuvered with my head on a swivel and scanned the skies for other aggressors I lost both the 190 and the 110. Neither had shown any further interest in me. I'll never know if the ME 110 made it home or not. I sure had laced him wing tip to wing tip ... but still couldn't claim a victory.

I did spot another lone Mustang homeward bound, wagged my wings and he joined me. It was Shorty Hanes of our squadron. He had knocked down a 110 and was exuberant. Obviously our 52nd Group found itself well scattered but had accomplished eight confirmed kills. Less fortunately we had lost two of our own to enemy fighters. My long-time buddy, Pappy Gross, had been one of our losses. Bullock and wingman, Grewe, shared a victory over a 110 and made it home. Shorty and I found three scattered returning bombers to escort back. I found Burns made it safely but as far as I was concerned his excuse for not sticking with me left serious questions.

Big Black Crosses

Most of our missions had proven less stressful than the Vienna run. But, on the very next dawning, we were unceremoniously rousted from the sack to escort heavies to the Ploesti oil fields. This would constitute a deep-reach and we anticipated that a formidable enemy reception would arise to protect its vital black gold. We guessed right.

Tyler again led our squadron but this time he was assigned group leader, in command of all three of the 52nd Group's Squadrons. I again led Tackle Yellow Flight with Burns on my wing and Bullock and Grewe rounding out our foursome. Primarily due to the wear and tear of back-to-back missions, we of the 4th Squadron lofted only twelve planes and by the designated time of rendezvous, two had returned due to mechanical troubles. Our bombers were late and we had to circle Budapest for a time. Tyler finally decided to hook up with a large group of B–17s whose fighter escorts were nowhere in sight.

Our 4th Squadron was flying mid-level cover. All was quiet for a spell but when the B–17s were not more than 40 miles from the target, we were shocked by a spectacular greeting. The garbled shouts in my earphones confirmed that the specter jarred almost everyone at once. A later official report stated that some 69 to 74 enemy fighter planes had approached us head on. Some were at our level. Some were slightly below … between us and the lower-level 5th Squadron. Most of us had never seen a close-up display of enemy force of this size in one gaggle. The first and most memorable communication blurted was, "Jesus! Big black crosses! The sky is full of them!"

In a flash, it was pandemonium. Orderliness of communications was the first to go with pilots shouting things like, "Break! Blue Two!" and with no squadron identifier. Multiple emotion-charged shouts cluttered the air in a cacophony ... "Watch your starboard Nick!" "Get the bastard Red three!" "109 coming in at three" "Look out Fred those 190's ... two o'clock low ... headin for the bombers!" The planes from the 2nd Squadron were diving through us. The guys from the 5th were climbing up midst us. An unseen power had stirred a seething maelstrom of both the enemy's and our airplanes.

I was bending the flight in a tight downward turn and heading for a couple of Focke-Wulf 190s that momentarily seemed unmolested. An even-closer 109 popped up ahead of us. I flicked a right climbing turn and the guy was just sitting there waiting to be had ... Just a little closer, steady, thumb on the trigger button and *Whaaa?* ... before I fired he popped the canopy and hit the silk. I nearly collided with him as he and his opening chute grazed by. I was in disbelief. Either his plane had already been hit or he was declaring his own private armistice. But no time for that, Bullock had called out three Macchi 205s moving toward us at 4 o'clock.

The Macchi 202 and the later 205 were both excellent fighters. They were designed and built by the Italians and were flown by the Germans or possibly Balkan fellow travelers. They didn't perform quite as well at high altitude as our P–51s or the latest German fighters. They were extremely maneuverable, however, and certainly tough at lower levels. The Macchis spotted us and turned away in a shallow dive. With Burns in tow, I pursued and was closing from about 7 o'clock on the lead plane while Bullock and Grewe scissored on the starboard 205. I got some strikes on the wings

Macchi MC – 202
Photo courtesy of
www.warbirdsresourcegroup.org

and Grewe got some fuselage hits on the other guy. All three enemy rolled over and split-s'ed vertically. We rolled over and down and kept close behind them.

Burns and Enemy Lose

Burns had been dancing around behind me. This behavior let me know he was champing at the bit. I guessed he felt that if he were in my place he would have finished the job sooner. On the other hand it was my flight and I knew I must do it my way. Also, he was distracting me with his flying ... like his bladder was full. Then it happened: The Macchis pulled out briefly, and with us closing once more they rolled over for a second time and dove straight for the deck.

I called, "Yellow Flight. Don't split-s. We can catch em."

I had glanced at my altimeter and airspeed and estimated that as we passed below 4,000 feet altitude, we might not have enough room to pull out of another vertical dive. The Macchis with their lower wing load-ing might make it.

I led a steep turning dive. Burns broke away from me, split-s'ed and closed on the tail of one the Macchis. As the Macchi pulled out, skimming the deck, it appeared Burns was getting strikes on him. Tragically, Burns was unable to pull up and hit the ground in a fireball. Bullock peppered the 205 ahead of him while it exploded in the trees. My adversary went into a tight turn just above the trees as I was closing. I followed and at this point, five or six other enemy fighters joined the melee.

Ring Around Rumania

I wound up in a circle as tight as I could pull it with at least two other Macchis behind me and the one ahead. Bullock and Grewe found themselves in the same position in a max tight turn with several other enemy planes. The enemy behind me was firing intermittent bursts at me and I was doing the same at the Macchi ahead of me in the circle. I realized I had made a big mistake getting into a low level turning contest with these Macchis. Also, I never expected to be dealing with this many fighters in the game. Somehow though, I was holding my own in the seemingly endless, unforgiving luftberry (circle).

The problem in hitting an opponent in the circle is that the shooter, in order to score, must aim well ahead of his target. The only way to do that, of course, is for the shooter to turn tighter than, or inside his opponent. So far no one in the circle had managed to do that. Every time I tried to tighten the turn my 51 would shutter and almost stall. That close to the ground a stall would be my last flying exhibition.

An irony of the luftberry is that he who flinches and turns out of the circle, with an opponent behind him, can be a fish in a barrel. In desperation, I pulled into so tight a turn that while I fired, my plane half stalled and the wing flicked. I thought I'd lost it. As I eased off to regain control the Macchi ahead in the luftberry abruptly snapped on his back, and smacked the brush in a violent, explosive disintegration.

I'll never know if I hit him or he made a low-level mistake of some kind. But finally I had a victory in the 51, albeit, not an easy one. Bullock witnessed the saga as our two circles of angry airplanes were intersecting. He and I had been trading terse comments on our predicaments throughout the ordeal. When my target splashed, the one nibbling at my tail and a third in the circle had, for some reason, turned and fled in opposite directions. I shouted something like, "Bullock! Let's hit the weeds! Wide open ... West!" With that, the three of us poked our noses down, regrouped and tickled the meadows for a minute or so. I made a climbing 180 degree turn for better position to re-engage whatever still lurked around. None of us could spot any airplanes.

Years later I would come across Bullock's diary of this encounter. He had written, "Boy, what a day this was. Had a mission to Ploesti. As we neared the target we encountered more enemy aircraft than I've ever seen before. All types ... 109s, 190s, MA205s, MA200s. Really a sight. Dogfights all over hell, fires, parachutes and what not. I was in McCampbell's flight. We got into a hell of a scrap with some ME205s. Mac go one; spun him in. I took a couple of 90 degree deflection shots. I didn't see anything, but Mac confirmed one for me when we got back. Said he blew all to hell. Tribbett got two, Tyler two, George one also. We lost Burns somewhere in the deal. The 2nd got five, 5th none, lost one each."

Our fight with the Macchis had carried us a distance to the east of Ploesti. No doubt we were too far from home with too little fuel for further chase. I felt thankful we had Pied-Pipered such a bunch of enemy fighters away from the bomber mission and, at least, destroyed two. The rest of the Macchis would have to refuel, re-climb to bomber altitude and find them. The bombers, by then, would be well on their way home and an unlikely intercept opportunity.

With Grewe on portside and Bullock on starboard, we began our climb back to altitude. For better coverage, we were flying line abreast with about 100 yards separation. Luckily, we had run on drop tank fuel till we jettisoned them back at onset of the enemy engagement. But I was devastated about Burns.

But the first order of business was to get busy with maps and begin looking for major landmarks. I had made enough trips over Southern Europe and the Balkans at high altitudes that I was familiar with major cities and rivers and their juxtapositions. Just give me some altitude, a reasonably clear day ... find Belgrade, for example, and home base is a shoo-in. My plan was for us to climb to about 28,000 feet and try to find some bombers heading home. I hadn't much hope of finding Tyler or any of the rest of the scattered squadron. I thought we could give maybe 15 or 20 minutes more protection time over some lonesome heavys before we leaned back our engines and made for the barn. I was ready for the haystack and a day off after my overdraft of adrenaline during these back-to-back workouts. But such plans and thoughts were grossly premature.

With my lap full of map, eyes scanning for landmarks and nearing 15,000 feet, Grewe blew my train of thought.

"Tackle Red One! Bandit 5 o'clock high! He's coming in!"

I cocked my head and saw what looked like an ME–109 heading for Bullock. Grewe and I contested the airway with shouts for Bullock to get ready to break. No response.

"Bullock, bandit Five o'clock!"

"He's coming in ... Fast!"

We both called and I waggled my wings and started a sharp climbing turn toward the intruder. "Break Right! Bullock! Break Right!" He didn't receive but he did start a turn as he saw us jerking right. It helped mess up the guy's aim on his first burst. But he was staying on Bullock's tail as he frantically turning inside-out trying to shake the enemy. This was one gutsy, hot shot, ME–109 cowboy with an initial advantage ... but seemingly alone.

By this time Bullock was finally audible and plaintively shouting, "God Mac! Get this bastard off my ass!" Over and over these exact words still echo through the years. I would never in my lifetime get a more compelling call. Here was my old flying school buddy and longtime sidekick, confidant and squadron mate ... Here was Bullock, a guy who would do anything for me ... and at this moment reaching for me to save his life.

With Grewe in tow I was frantically squirming to get inside the 109's arc while he was firing from inside Bullock's. I finally managed to get awkwardly behind the bastard and in the turn I was squirting short bursts at him. But again, couldn't get enough lead. *If only this airplane would bend in the middle!* I'm sure, however, I was making that 109 jockey damned nervous as he looked over his shoulder.

Can't say I didn't have enough practice that day on deflection shots. As it was with the Macchis, I kicked the rudder mercilessly, I pulled the stick in tighter than felt good. I squeezed out a long burst with more than one ring-sight lead. My airplane completely shielded my view of the adversary while I fired. I could see Bullock ahead, and prayerfully un-hit ... then remarkably, as I relaxed slightly from the stalling turn, the enemy fighter broke away from the fight ... inverted and nosed into heavy clouds. I had seen no strikes, but Grewe said, "Hell, I think you hit him bad, Mac! He broke off flying crazy and smokin' like a chimney!" Grewe and I, with Bullock moving up fast, had only a moment's, cloudy chase as the 109 disappeared.

Fuel was becoming too much of a concern for continued pursuit. Bullock had mentioned that he'd gathered some 109-sponsored holes in his wings as souvenirs. So with some incidental recap chatter we three reformed and made directly for home without further incident.

The unexpected anti-climax to all this, for me, came a couple of days later during the viewing of gun camera film from the mission with the assembled 52nd Group pilots. This was a regular and exciting ritual following film development of the most recent action. My film of the duel with the 109 which had attacked Bullock included a surprise. It was unanimously agreed that my film clearly showed fatal hits on the ME–109 cockpit. The gun camera had captured a view I could only see on film. Gun cameras were triggered to roll with the fighters' gunfire and had an automatic overrun of a few seconds after the gun trigger was released.

The cockpit obviously had been peppered and emblazoned while hidden from my observation. The rule was that since no one had witnessed the plane crash or explode, I could only claim a probable. Today a film clip print of that 109's certain fate hangs in our den with a collection of my WWII photos, including those of Bullock, McCauley *et al.*

The Tally

The loss of Burns was an especially tragic one for me. I agonized over the possibility that I could have done a better job of training him. On the positive side I must add that our 4th Squadron of ten participating pilots had, on this mission, chalked up seven confirmed victories plus one probably destroyed and four damaged. Tyler had downed two. Damned if Tribbett hadn't bagged two, Goettleman one and, of course, Bullock and I one confirmed each. Naturally I always insist the total number of enemy destroyed was clearly eight. I could possibly stretch it to nine. No one ever claimed the additional enemy loss of the fighter whose pilot deserted it in midair, early in the fight.

McCampbell's gun camera view
Courtesy of Bob McCampbell

Perch with a View

Toward the end of June we began to exchange our P–51Bs and Cs for the bubble-canopy Ds. They were the more esthetic P–51s and the darlings of post war air shows, air races and WWII airplane memorabilia. No question they were beautiful fighters and an improvement over their predecessors. Improved visibility was the primary step-forward feature. And ability to see the surroundings was certainly high on the fighter pilots' priority list.

Strangely enough, the old buggies with their bird cage canopies were five or ten miles per hour faster than their more glamorous new half brothers. We were still excited to have the new Ds. The easy panoramic view from the bubble presented a whole new world out there. I'll have to admit that I was beginning to question just how much more of that world from the cockpit I needed to see.

July and the new Ds started out as a busy month of escort missions but produced little "write home about" action. According to my flight log, from the 2nd through the 9th, I flew five more long ones but recall little about them.

Lost in a Puff of Smoke

What I can remember is that the escort flights continued to be arduous. Just being incarcerated in that small cocoon for five or six hours was punishment enough for one's sins. Although the poor bomber guys were much more vulnerable than we, several hours of flinching at bursts of flak wasn't easy on our nerves either. After an hour or so, each time your constantly panning eyes passed a minute smudge on the bubble, your heart let you know it had additional beats to spare. After all, an early spotting of an enemy plane could be a life-saver.

I do recall that it was on one of these early July runs that we suffered a rare loss to high altitude flak. We had visited the vast Ploesti oil plantation again and I had been leading the squadron escorting B–24s. We had been operating as top cover at almost 29,000 feet, far above the normal flak bursting levels encountered by the bombers. Startlingly, several unusually large caliber bursts had exploded amidst us. They had to have been radar-directed.

"Tackle Blue One, Blue Four here ... Think I've been hit, ... Losing coolant"

"Tackle Red One, Tackle Blue here. Yeah, Blue Four is streaming glycol."

"Tackle Blue Four, send Blue Three with Four. Blue three, keep altitude west. Blue Four if engine seizes, better the hit silk about 10K. Good luck Ed."

A relatively new addition to our squadron, Ed Turner, was hit in a coolant line by a piece of flak. He was seen safely landing by chute. But Rumania was a long way from home. All I could think of at the time was *God, what a tragic and unlikely fluke!*

Chapter 11

The Color of First
Class Americans

As Cleopatra famously said to Mark Anthony,
"I'm not prone to argue!"

Lieutenant Colonel Bob Levine, our group
commander, passed the happy word.
Tribbett, Bullock and I, along with three guys each
from the 2nd and 5th Squadrons, were invited to accompany him on a ten-day rest leave to Egypt.

A twin engine B–25 attached to the group had
become Levine's excursion airliner of choice. Levine
and a 2nd Squadron pilot took the driver's seats, leaving the rest of us sandbagged in the waist of the uncomfortable bomber-bird. Could you believe we were
anxiously piling on for a busman's holiday in the form
of a long, butt-burning flight?

To start our vacation, we lost an engine on takeoff and barely struggling back to base for a safe landing. *God! After lucking out on over 70 combat runs, am
I gonna get mine on the way to a vacation?* At least the
two days it took for the engine change gave us time to
wash and dry our skivvies. On the third day we were
airborne again for Cairo.

We cruised down the Italian boot, across the
Mediterranean and eastward over the Libyan Desert.
About sixty miles east of Alexandria, Egypt lay El
Alamein, the site of the British Army's stunning and
decisive victory in the fall of 1942 over Rommel, the
Desert Fox. Peering out of the portside window of the

B–25, I could see the remnants of that classic battle arrayed for miles but only partially protruding from the sand. The opposing tanks, artillery, lorries and armored vehicles were still lined up like a toy war game abandoned in the dirt.

We landed at Cairo Airport where a joint British and U.S. command arrangement prevailed. After piling out of the plane with our gear and hailing a lorry, we were confronted by a British officer and his MPs at the gate. He promptly saluted Levine and called him aside for a brief discussion. Levine walked back and facing us asked, "You guys don't want to stay anywhere you gotta wear ties, do you?" It was a quick and unanimous, "No Sir!" Levine turned back to the Brit, returned his second salute and added, "Cheerio!"

Bartender? An Alexander, Please?

As he led us back toward the plane, Levine shot another question, "How about we try a stay in Alexandria? Hear it's a great spot." We all agreed, took off and in no time circled the city. From what we could see it was a beautiful seaside resort. And we weren't wrong. We stayed there the entire eight or nine incredibly relaxing days. There seemed to be everything to meet a young man's fancy: beaches, restaurants, terrific night club entertainment, country clubs, horse racing and, yes, girls.

Like Capri, the city lured Europeans of means, who could afford to sit out the war in this spa. There were very few U.S. military in evidence, but uniformed British soldiers were frequently seen.

You could buy almost any appliance, un-rationed gas, steaks, top liquor brands: All the luxury things unavailable in the wartime U.S., or the rest of the world. The wealthy occupied posh beach homes or multiple dwelling condo-like, shoreline villas. There were many up-scale apartment buildings throughout the city. It was hard to imagine that Rommel had been knocking at Alexandria's door, only sixty miles away.

In Egypt's coastal Mediterranean playground we found ourselves enjoying a completely decadent, relaxing break from the war. Alexandria's nightclubs offered well-staged and well-performed, Las Vegas-like song, dance and comedy entertainment that would be applauded anywhere. Bullock, Trib and I got rooms in a small hotel right on a good beach with surprisingly decent waves for the Mediterranean. The rooms were small but had indoor plumbing. This was clearly an upgrade from our three-or-four-pilots-to-a-tent suites and our three-seats-to-an-outhouse accommodations back in Italy.

Reach Partner!

With all the fun we ugly Americans enjoyed, I did have one sobering experience. I met a seemingly sophisticated and certainly pretty little blond French girl about my age. We struck up a conversation in a department store. Her name was Monique and she lived with her parents in a downtown apartment. This was not a New York penthouse, but a typical, average-income, city-dweller abode of the time. The family had traveled a lot and she had grown up accumulating seven European languages, and English.

She really knew her way around Alexandria and around the ubiquitous Yankee dollar chasers. This attribute saved me some piasters when out on the town. Ironically, she loved horse racing and this activity quickly eliminated any cost advantage she offered. One night I had taken Monique home from dinner and a show. We had hailed a horse and buggy from wherever we'd been. Bidding her adieu, I began strolling down the street past some paranoia-provoking Egyptians, bistros and habitats.

I decided it the better part of valor to flag a cab instead of being discriminated against as a foreigner in a foreign land. The cab turned out to be as seedy as the surroundings. There was another indigenous sort beside the driver in the front seat. The driver took a bit of a circuitous route to my hotel and I had commented thereon. Finally he pulled up to the curb near the entrance. The streets were dark and empty.

I began opening the car door and asking about the fare. The other guy was getting out too. The driver then announced the amount owed which was a good twenty times the going rate. I said, "No, "Six piasters!" The driver exited and stepped quickly around behind me. Both began inching closer and the driver had begun pointing toward my wallet. In my right hand leather jacket pocket, I regularly carried a small Italian Beretta pistol, and I grabbed for it. Simultaneously, the robe-and-turban-garbed hotel bellboy, who slept on an outside cot at our hotel entrance, was awakened and quickly jumped to his feet.

Saved by a Terrorist?

This bellboy was a massive, almost seven-foot giant, who never said much. He just hung around outside the hotel and watched over it. He moved fast for a guy who never seemed to move at all. He hovered over the three of us like a giant brooding eagle. I backed off and the eagle showed his talons casting some angry Arabic at the two cabbies. Their replies failed to adequately answer his questions.

He suddenly grabbed both cabbies and stuffed them back into the cab while shouting more Arabic. He seemed to be saying something like, "And if I ever catch you infidels around here again, I'll bust up your cab and other more personal items." Upon our Alexandria departure, I left him a rather large tip. They say that a fighter pilot's downfall is fast planes, fast women and slow horses. *Au revoir*, Monique.

A Gin Run and the Brewmeister Delivers

We popped onto the Island of Cypress on the way home and loaded the B–25 with a few cases of Cypress gin. The payload in bomb bays can sometimes deliver joy as well as distress to its recipients.

Back home at Madna with the rites of summer in full swing, we scarcely had enough ice for cold beer ... let alone a gin and tonic. When we began receiving individual beer rations in the spring of 1944, necessity became the mother of invention. The innovative refrigeration recipe called for a pilot, a P–51 and two modified drop-tanks. The aircraft maintenance crew had crafted a hinged door on the tanks. Loading them on a Mustang and filling each with cans of beer, the Brewmeister would hop into the P–51 climb to 30,000 feet, cruise around at that altitude for 30 or 40 minutes and dive back with the cold beer ... to the waiting applause of his squadron-mates. Some self-styled physicist amongst us must have given the pilots specific time-at-altitude parameters to avoid costly over-cooling disasters. Never crossed my mind at the time, but this refrigeration system must have been a mite pricey at today's gasoline prices.

I flew several more escort missions during the fading days of July 1944. One was notably different from the others in that we escorted some gutsy guys flying C–47 transports. It seems that the Yugoslav underground had worked out a system whereby they would take over an under-manned airstrip from the Germans. They would hold it long enough so that downed and evading Allied airmen who had been rounded up throughout the Balkans could be evacuated. The escorted C–47s would land at the airstrip, load the evacuees on the run and within minutes were off with the precious cargo on the return trip to Italy.

By this time, the Germans were extremely hard-pressed to hold on to their occupation of Yugoslavia. We did look for targets of opportunity while on these

rescue missions, but it was extremely tough to dis-
tinguish good guys from bad in that terrain. On one
of these sweeps a C–47 returned a pilot of another
nearby fighter group who had been downed and had
evaded capture for several months. With help of indigenous partisans and while listed as an MIA, he had
walked back from eastern Rumania, a distance of well
over 500 miles. The soles of his tough GI boots were
long gone from his arduous, harrowing trek to the
Yugoslavian bus stop.

Dis-integration

One day in July 1944, McCauley led me on a
short, but unforgettable, adventure that showcased
my nation's own racial intolerance. I had been raised
in an atmosphere emphasizing that our Constitution
was for everyone. Not that discrimination failed to ex-
ist, in my California youth, but at least our education

McCauley, me and my "51"
Photo courtesy of Bob McCampbell

and sports were integrated, as were our buses, restrooms and water fountains. The African American population in California was then indeed small. Now it just followed that McCauley, a true southerner, and I had been an Odd Couple in respect to the racial question. He occasionally referred to me as a nigger-lover and on those occasions I called him "Massa."

Ironically, it was none other than Jimmy McCauley who decided he would pay a social call on the boys of the all-African American 332nd Fighter Group now famed as the Tuskegee Airmen ... and like us, flying P–51 Mustangs. What's more, he invited me to accompany him, which made me feel obligated but a little uneasy. It seemed that while I had always professed a strong advocacy for equal rights, I had to admit I'd really never done much toward advancing that goal. After all, what did I know about African Americans? McCauley's youth, necessarily, had included continual contact with black America.

The airfield of the 332nd was located only about twenty miles down the Adriatic coast from us. McCauley drove the jeep down the mostly dusty roads and our conversation touched on our homes, wives and families whom we had left behind for well more than a year. Naturally, we veered from such rather painful nostalgia to talk a bit about where we were going on this day and why. The why was the best question. For me, I guess it was curiosity. As we drove on I realized curiosity was also why McCauley was so interested. But his was focused somewhat differently. McCauley needed to see, first hand, how blacks could possibly fly the world's hottest and most technologically advanced airplanes ... how they could handle the flying and leadership requirements necessary to meet the challenges of the air war over Europe ... and just what kind of folks were these airmen anyway? It just seemed unlikely from his social nurturing that blacks could measure up to the job.

Questions like these were the ones the U.S. military and Congress had been debating since the Army Air Corps had only reluctantly admitted the first black flying cadets in 1941. Like all black American recruits, these selectees had remained segregated throughout the war. This policy had prevailed through their training in Tuskegee, Alabama, their commissioning as U.S. Army officers, their combat deployment overseas and their return to duty in the states. It was at some point after our hosts had been posted to combat duty overseas that a rather heated congressional hearing had taken place. Raised during the hearing was the question as to whether or not to discontinue the Tuskegee program. A more disturbing proposal of withdrawing the 332nd from combat was voiced. All sorts of accusations were hurled, including reports alleging everything from incompetence to cowardice in combat.

Luckily, Lt. Colonel Benjamin Davis Jr. an iron-willed West Point graduate and first African American military pilot, had brought eloquence and evidence to counter the accusations. With the aid of a few sympathetic congressmen and white military officials, the accusations were eventually dropped. Davis had led this first black unit (the one we were to visit) into combat, and had since testified stateside and returned from the hearings. The unit had been deployed in North Africa at about the time McCauley and I arrived there in May 1943. Regrettably, Col. Davis was attending a meeting during our visit to his outfit.

So as we paused at the gate of the 332nd Fighter Group on a balmy Italian summer afternoon in July of 1944, a young lieutenant met us in another jeep and escorted us down the flight line of red-tailed Mustangs. We stopped by his personal plane for a moment, as he proudly pointed out his girlfriend's name, "Bell", boldly inscribed on the nose. We spent a few minutes talking with him and his crew chief and were then whisked off to the officers mess. This accommodation was a single story framed, rectangular, tarpaper building much like ours and repeated by the Army by the tens of thousands at temporary military sites in the U.S. and around the world.

We walked through the dining area into a make-shift bar where six or seven pilots were enjoying cocktails around a large oval table. Our host, the lieutenant, introduced us to his squadron mates, including a captain, their squadron CO. The conversation was a little awkward at first. I suppose neither they, nor we, had enjoyed any informal inter-social gatherings akin to this anywhere in military life. The system of segregation just didn't allow it to happen.

It now seems so surreal. Here we were, brothers in a highly specialized and supposedly integrated military operation, facing a common foe, with weapons in common and in a common arena. We were about the same age and faced identical military challenges, fears and aspirations. If ever a scenario was devised that demanded the closest bonds among men, this had to be it. And finally, what were we fighting for anyway? Weren't we a unity of free peoples bound together against a powerful tyranny, a force that was bent on world domination and who preached and practiced social injustice?

The conversation relaxed as we inevitably moved it into talk of airplanes, mission experiences, mutual feelings and all those myriad of fighter pilot things that clearly did bond us.

As we moved from the bar to the mess hall, some of our hosts' conversation impressed me by their general sophistication and quality of expression. I remember this impression also caught McCauley's attention and retention. Looking back, many of these men were simply better educated than either of us. The standards for their selection had been relatively high. All in all, the visit had amounted to an enjoyable and instructive outing but much too short an evening for us both. We had been treated hospitably and they seemed to have genuinely welcomed our visit.

We thanked our hosts and jeeped back to our base catching the last rays of daylight. It was an experience not easily tossed aside and I'm sure McCauley, as well as I, returned with a bundle of afterthoughts. The obvious question bugging me was how these men could reconcile putting their lives on the line in the cause of freedom and justice when they had enjoyed so little themselves. These precious inalienable rights had been compromised even while they were engaged in the fighting. Among other things, it was impossible for us, at the close of our stay, to offer our hosts a reciprocal visit to our squadron and I'm sure they knew it. How, under such conditions, which were compounded by unjust criticism, had they sustained the

Captain Armour McDaniels gets Hole-in-One ... Mustang
Photo courtesy of Bob McCampbell

high level of morale they so clearly exhibited?

But just how competent were these Tuskegee Airmen? Although they'd taken enough slings and arrows to evoke a congressional hearing, they received enough plaudits in the post war literature to credit them with being almost super-human. We did have some personal experience in flying on some of the same missions as they. We'd noted their red tails frequently while heading out and returning from missions. We'd listened to their chatter of communications and our paths had crossed over the target areas. We'd read commendatory reports from the bombers they escorted and from other fighter groups with whom they had danced the enemy skies. While inevitably one would hear the occasional voice of a detractor, the outpouring of praise for the competence and accomplishments of the 332nd was overwhelming.

Whether judged from behind a rifle or a stick and rudder pedals, the answer undoubtedly lay in the eyes of the beholder. To me, it was obvious that those who expected incompetence, or shameful performance by African Americans, always felt they found it. At the other extreme some apologists may have exaggerated Tuskegee heroics. On behalf of the record, however there's no question that the Tuskegee pilots downed their share of enemy fighters. Moreover, apparently no outfit out-performed the 332nd in preventing losses of our bombers to opposing fighters. In my experience, they were simply another gathering of young American flyers who certainly performed as well as any of us. Their steadfast dedication to duty under a heavy burden of prejudicial treatment would clearly seem to make them more deserving of applause than most. The Tuskegee Airmen unquestionably did a job to make a nation proud.

Chapter 12

To Russia with Shove

Nothing Like a Day Off

On the 4th of August 1944, I was in a deep sleep, secure in the privacy of my mosquito netting, oblivious to loud voices disturbing the serenity of the pre-dawn hours. When it was not my day to fly I conditioned myself to tune out such goings on within my tent until the perpetrators had departed for breakfast. I had planned my day, no strict schedule.

A typical off-day schedule would include relaxing over a cup of coffee, a habit that wasn't bladder friendly on days featuring a five or six hour mission. I would then head out on foot to the nearby travelogue shores of the Adriatic to immerse myself in its therapeutic waters and spend the morning swimming, sunning and writing letters home. I'd nap after lunch, maybe do some laundry and before dinner, drink a couple of beers with the boys. Finally, I would settle in with a book and get a good sleep before the next day's mission.

Day Off in the USSR?

Well, guess what happened on the way to a day of relaxation? First thing, Tribbett startles me awake.

"Mac! Mac!" You gotta wake up! We got a special mission! You gotta take it!"

"You're kidding, Trib. This is my day off."

"Mac we've a mission to Russia ... Russia, Mac! Tyler's gone. I got a damned cold. If I could do it I would. You're the only one to take the squadron. You have to roll Mac! Not much time. Big briefing in thirty minutes. Damned, I'm sorry Mac."

Tim Tyler, our squadron CO, had gone on a few days leave. Tim and the 2nd Squadron CO had taken their Mustangs on a flight to visit newly liberated Paris. As I climbed toward the east wearing Tyler's shoes, I thought, 'great timing Tim'. At a squadron reunion many years later, Tim had jokingly agonized. "Damned you Mac! You got to take my squadron on the Russian run. I been kicking myself in the butt for that ever since."

I tossed a frown of disappointment at Trib and glanced over at my tentmate, Fred Bullock "Grab your socks Mac," says he, leaping out of his cot and reaching for his flight suit. It dawned on me that he was already scheduled to fly. At least this cast one comforting note on the fast-deteriorating original format for my day.

Tribbett explained that the mission was just sent down from Wing Headquarters the night before. The guys in group were still frantically preparing my revised day. Among other things, special escape kits had to be readied for each pilot. These contained cash, morphine shots, small rubber encased hacksaws (to conceal up your butt, if captured), identification photos in peasant garb (to use for forged IDs), maps printed on rubberized silk handkerchiefs, a mini-compass, and more, all tailored to the countries we might be visiting ... accidentally. Each pilot was also furnished with appropriate aerial maps.

The squadron leaders were issued specially constructed strip-maps. These were cut about six inches in width with each sequential map of the mission route taped to the next. In this manner the strip could be unfolded as we progressed and they avoided a blanketing of the cockpit with opened full sized maps. The route, rendezvous points, times and other information were marked in bold pen. This worked pretty well as long as you didn't wander off the path of the strip coverage. Of course, the squadron leader had a set of full area maps as well. He often inked certain abbreviated mission data on the palm of his hand or glove or maybe on a note taped to his flight suit knee.

The briefing room was a buzzing cacophony of comment. We stood at attention as Levine came up front and greeted us. He apologized for the short lead-time and turned around the large portable blackboard on stage. Sure enough, here exposed, was a map showing a dark line reaching from our air strip on the Italian Adriatic, across the Balkans, to somewhere in the USSR. There were wows and other exclamations even though most of us had gotten a strong hint. "Yep," says Levine, "We're providing cover for the 82nd Group's P–38s hitting airfields along the Russian front." The 4th Squadron would do top cover. This was a switch ... fighters protecting other fighters?

The briefing was short because of time constraints. The intelligence guy briefed that we could encounter relatively strong resistance from German fighters. No one was surprised at that. This guy also admonished us not to involve ourselves in political discussions with the Russians. The weather forecaster was so full of possibilities you could have your choice. It seemed to me this mission had great potential for some screw-ups. After picking up our escape kits and maps, I got our guys together around my airplane for a quick Q&A session. Then we mounted our thoroughbreds, I signaled an engine start and we were off.

Who Needs Unsolicited Flak?

We met the P–38s right on time just west of Ploesti, Rumania. We all figured they would be circumventing the vast refinery area and thus avoid its equally vast anti-aircraft defenses. But no! They were sailing right for hell's thousand acres. I could hear Major Fuller, the 5th squadron CO, who was also our group leader, as he profanely announced he was sharply turning away. The leader of the 2nd squadron, Captain Schnieder and I followed suit with our squadrons. The skies surrounding the leading squadron of P-38s were suddenly overcast with anti aircraft bursts. The airwaves were quickly and predictably filled with shouts of the P-38 pilots such as, "Lets get the hell out of here!" and some other words they perhaps learned from Major Fuller. I saw one P-38 go down smoking. It was a senseless mistake to needlessly cruise that area at relatively low altitude.

This mistake also led to another problem. The P-38s became scattered and we were beginning to run into cloud layers. There was one layer about 2,000 feet above us, which I didn't like a bit. There was another gradually thickening layer about 3,000 feet below. I was quickly losing visual contact with the P-38s and I could no longer pick out any of our other group aircraft. I called Major Fuller and suggested we drop down to about the level of and behind the 2nd squadron. "Roger Tackle One." Came the reply. I had decided to drop through the lower cloud level very carefully since it was hard to guess where all the other aircraft were positioned. With map in lap again I started to advise my squadron members as to our immanent let-down.

Ambushed!

My train of thought was shattered ...

"109s! Tackle, break left!" someone screamed.

More calls exploded into my headset.

"Break!"

"Get the fudder!"

"Coming through at five!"

"Yellow Three, take the other bastard!"

"Red Four drop tanks!"

"I hit the SOB!"

Ten 109s and five 190s had struck us almost at dead astern from out of the upper cloud layer. Our drop tanks were tumbling free. The enemy attackers split every direction, as did most of my squadron. Bullock's wingman, Ben Stewart, was hit and coolant was streaming from his engine. Bullock advised him to bail.

One extroverted 109 pilot, apparently the squadron leader, buzzed right over my canopy and inexplicably performed a victory slow roll. Of all times, I was struggling with a reluctant drop–tank, which finally tumbled free. He pulled up almost into an Immelmann (a maneuver in which an airplane reverses direction by executing half of a loop upwards followed by half of a roll called also Immelmann turn) and down, turning in the direction of another pass at me or nearby Wiley. I had already anticipated his direction. His turn had taken him a bit wide due to his speed. I was able to cut inside his turn as he took a deflection shot at Wiley. I fired a burst at the attacker.

I thought I hit this grandstander when he snapped over, breaking away from Wiley. As he dove for the lower cloud level I followed behind, in a diving turn with those 12 Packard Rolls cylinders pounding at max. He straightened out his dive and I got another good bead on him from almost dead astern. Just a tad of a ring lead ... "There! Hotshot SOB!" Hits splashed along the starboard side of the engine and wing ... Bingo! The 109 erupted in flame as it entered the clouds. Wiley and my wingman, Fitzpatrick, reported him a confirmed destroyed.

The entire engagement probably took only a couple of minutes. Bullock, Gassman, Frye and

Montgomery of our squadron each scored hits on separate 109s before the scattered enemy attackers evaporated into the overcast. Fitzpatrick got strikes on a Focke-Wulf 190 who was working to get behind me. Stewart, sadly, had also disappeared through clouds during the skirmish. He insisted we not worry and that he would get out OK. I hoped the calm following our furious melee wasn't an eye of the storm.

The loss of Stewart gnawed at my conscience. Damned! The Huns must have been directed on our butts by radar. The only thing unbelievably positive about the engagement was that we'd lost no one else. At least this seemed to be so from all observations and communications. I could have wasted a moment in revelry over my aerial conquest, but there were much higher priorities.

Roundup

First I had to corral the scattered Mustangs. There had been some improvement in ceiling and visibility as I got down to about 5,000 feet. This was just beyond the eastern down slopes of the Carpathian Mountains. I could see what I thought must be one of German airfields that had been targeted by the P–38s. It lay ten or fifteen miles to the north of me. Some structures and probably planes on the ground were still burning. There was a fairly sizable town toward the southeast, located on a large river running north and south. It looked like the Prut River on my map.

Wiley and Deckman formed up with me after my 109 incident. Bullock and the remaining six squadron guys, fortunately, got themselves together at some point. I advised them of my coordinates, altitude and visual position. I added that the three of us would be circling there for five minutes. I told Bullock that he was in charge, if we failed to rendezvous in the time allotted. We all remained in radio contact, which meant we weren't separated by too many miles. Time had halted as we approached the four-minute mark.

It was Deckman who called with unmistakable glee. "Red One! I see them! Two o'clock level!" I hoped the "them" was our guys ... not more of the black crosses. Miraculously, it was our good guys, every one. What a remarkable relief to be reunited in that vast area ... one so unfamiliar to any of us.

Still Gets Lonely Out Here on the Prairie

The P–38s had long gone. No sign or calls from the other 52nd Group Squadrons. During our engagement I had exchanged a few terse words on our situation with the group leader, Major Fuller. Radio patter from the strafing P–38 pilots had rightly crowded the airwaves, but strangely enough our inter-squadron communications had rapidly evaporated, without even a ... "Are you having a nicer day now?" "Or "Do you need help?" No question, we were well separated from the rest of the force. In fact, scatter was soon to emerge as this mission's name.

We lofted only twelve airplanes from our squadron at the start. As we began our initial climb east over the Adriatic, I allowed Lieutenant Parent, a new addition to the squadron roster, to turn back with a rough engine. Now with Stewart missing, our total squadron force was down to ten airplanes. Wiley, a major from the Training Command, was recently assigned from the states and this, of all missions, would be his first. Wiley had wound up with a flight of only two airplanes, due to a last minute mechanical scrub and Parent's early return.

How About a Pay Raise, Boss?

I considered the other 4th Squadron guys on this Russia Run to be well seasoned. Each had weathered a busy month or so with us. Major Wiley clearly possessed good insight and flying skill. He even took me aside, prior to the mission, to say that if I held any doubts, I would be his squadron leader in all respects and that he would appreciate any advice I could offer now or in the course of the mission. Although I felt I understood my position, it was an unusual military command situation. So I appreciated his reassuring confidence in me.

On the other hand, I would've have been more confident had Wiley possessed combat time comparable to the others. With this in mind, I had once again buried my head in my accordion strip-map. It had nearly blinded me, when tossed against the canopy from the sudden contorted pursuit of the ME-109.

Where's Magellan When You Need Him

Our destination was Poltava, a small city located about 150 miles west southwest of Kiev. It was starting to rain hard and visibility was diminishing. We dropped about 2,000 feet trying to stay under the cloud cover and trying to identify landmarks. In those days the iron beam was the fighter pilot's navigational system of preference. This meant finding a railroad track and following it to a city. If no track, we matched the hills, the windmills, the roads, the towns and the rivers on our aviation maps with those on the ground. If all else failed, we had been exposed to some academics in celestial navigation and done some instrument training, which was considered flying blind.

The trouble was, our training had been too accelerated and the instruments too primitive. It's no secret that fighter pilots generally tried to avoid getting into instrument flying situations. Fortunately, my first inclination to use the old iron beam system worked. I located what appeared to be the Ukrainian City of Chisinau. If so, we would be nearing the Russo-German battle lines along the Dniester River.

Now down to about 1,000 feet the limited visibility, due to rain, was beginning to make abandonment of the iron beam navigation system a worthy consideration. At higher altitude clouds and rain obscured the landscape ... an essential ingredient of the iron beam system. Besides there wasn't a railroad track going our way and we risked running into an immovable object while flying that low. We had glimpsed at what could have been the Dniester River and a bunch of men and equipment doing things that armies do.

Climbing Out

With this precise location information I advised the squadron that we would have to climb on top of the front and navigate by time and distance until we ran into a break in the weather. We tightened our formation into a "V" so each pilot could see another just ahead. This would keep the squadron from scattering in the blind climb. We then climbed up through the guck on instruments. A gremlin was holding back the hands of my watch as I sweated that assent. Finally, we popped out, at almost 30,000 feet, into the brilliant sunshine. What a sight, what a contrast, what a relief to have the squadron together, dancing over the endless sun bleached clouds.

Another Fine Mess the Army's ...

At least I could now read the fine stuff on my maps. But whoa! That otherwise welcome advantage of legibility had only left me baffled by what I read ... or what I didn't read. My short-lived, sun-inspired euphoria had vanished. I tried to find the Dniester on my strip map. I had written this river on my crib notes of check points on my left palm. I thought I had read Dniester on the strip map as identifying the river on the Russo-German front. I thought this had been the one we had seen when we started our climb to the sunshine. Now, I find that the only river named, in the region where I thought the Dniester ought to be, was its phonetic cousin, the River Dnieper.

In my stream of consciousness, the River Dnieper (not Dniester) was to be our last big check point before reaching our destination, Poltava. We just couldn't have past this last landmark (Dnieper) so soon. I had figured another 300 miles to go for that. Good grief!

It took some frantic moments of map study and it hit me. Group headquarters had, in its mad Russian rush, omitted an entire map section from my strip maps. In this crazy environment, I wasn't dead sure about my conclusion but I decided I had no choice but to do it my way and pray for the Dnieper to show up in the next hour.

Wiley's Mistake a Blessing?

Each of the guys had given me remaining fuel estimates. An hour's worth had been about average. Typically, some had less, some figured a little more. Wiley, while checking his, had noticed his oxygen level was dangerously low. The oxygen regulator could be set on either demand or emergency. The regulator was always set on demand except in certain rare circumstances. Prompted by changes in altitude, the demand system doled out oxygen as physiologically needed above 10,000 feet. If set on emergency, the system rendered the oxygen flow wide open and depleted the supply in a much shorter time. Wiley had mistakenly set his system on emergency .So rather than abandon Wiley to a lonely, low altitude flight where no oxygen was required ... nothing for me to do but drop the whole squadron back down through the overcast.

We had been flying on top for about fifteen minutes. It would have been necessary to let down eventually. Another half hour at altitude, however, would certainly have saved some fuel. Further, I hoped to find, at some point, a break in the weather.

At any rate, down we went and rather rapidly for Wiley's sake. At 5,000 feet, we still hadn't broken out of the clouds. That was disappointing but, flying in heavy overcast for any distance would make it tough to keep a group of fighters together. At very low altitudes at least some terrain was perceptible as were nearby airplanes. But, lousy weather at low altitudes was a navigational nightmare and posed hazards from tall fixed objects.

Even though most of the southern Ukraine is decorated with monotonous flat wheat fields, we continued our let down, but now more cautiously. We began seeing the deck at about 2,000 feet. Not much had changed since we had left it. Not enough ceiling to navigate without a real iron beam and a known terminal. Compounding the whole affair was continued heavy rain and no landmarks other than large, lake-sized puddles.

Navigational Guestimate Alive and Well

I continued my heading east. What better, when you're looking for a very large river in that direction, especially one that runs north and south ... most of the time. God! I could be anywhere within a 200 mile radius. Another 30 minutes to go and then, by my reckoning ... the river Dnieper (if all my other estimates and my hunch that I was missing a map section were right). Every piece of real estate is an instant replay. Waiting to see the river was driving me insane. I wondered what my squadron mates were thinking? Probably, "Does Mac know what the hell he's doing? "Or Christ, doesn't he know we're going to have to ditch these things in the wheat pretty soon?"

The next fuel check didn't help the atmosphere much. I had visions of a court martial for losing the entire squadron to the Russian breadbasket. I tried to think of some positive things in my defense.

> *After all, hadn't our squadron been the only outfit to chase off the only sizable enemy air opposition encountered? Hadn't we been the epitome of mission fulfillment, i.e., protected the sheep from the wolves?*

The prosecuting officer was just going into a rebuttal of my testimony with something like, "Lt. McCampbell, if the enemy had jumped the P–38s, was it at all likely the enemy could not have downed as many P–38s as the number of P–51s you were responsible for losing in a wheat field?"

Lost and Found

My daydream wake-up call had begun to interrupt the prosecuting officer's case against me. Back in the real world, we had spent our 30 minutes wisely, that is, we were all still in the air and together. The next five minutes had been the longest yard. My tired eyes had visited nothing but Ukrainian puddles that had expanded into water, water everywhere. I was worried that if we did see a large body of water, no one would recognize it as a river. Gratefully, the visibility was improving a bit allowing us to gain a little more altitude ... And voila! There it (or some river) surely was! It was several miles wide ... wider in spots. I called, "Tackle Squadron, Red One here, 90 starboard."

My plan had been to fly south down the Dnieper, wherever along it we might be. The map had indicated several large towns on the way toward Dnepropetrovsk. This was a significant port city on the river, down in the direction of the Black Sea. I knew there was a major Russian airport there but a little out of our fuel range. At least I was back on a map again, having flown in a storm for about 300 miles without one.

We didn't fly for more than a few minutes when we came upon a town that couldn't have owned a better landmark. The river had been dammed and suddenly narrowed at this point. I began to circle the squadron over what looked to be a place on the map called Kremenchug.

One sweep around the place without finding an airstrip was as disappointing as it gets. I resumed our flight plan down the river while entertaining calls of fuel estimates. "Red one, Red Two here. Got less than 10 minutes left." But just as the prosecutor was resuming his case, Bullock hollers, "Mac! They're shooting flares back there!" I wheeled us back around in a direction just west of the city and we looked closely. There rested a grass airfield that had blended in perfectly with all the rest of the Ukraine. On it were a couple of small buildings, some tents, a bunch of camouflaged American-loaned P–40s, and best of all, some uniformed men standing next to a wind sock and waving.

Let's Do Lunch Sometime, Ivor

We had no radio communication so I buzzed the field with my landing gear down and peeled up and around to the downwind leg. Then everyone landed in close-sequence on the wide meadow with wingmen almost lined abreast. Two Russian soldiers on a motorcycle and sidecar directed us to parking spots. As I climbed from my plane, a Soviet officer hopped out of an American Jeep. I didn't know his rank, but I immediately saluted and offered a handshake.

No one on the field spoke any English, which contributed to the initial awkwardness of the situation. On the other hand our hosts couldn't have been friendlier. In retrospect, it was incredible how well we communicated on a variety of topics. For example, the Russian pilots were fascinated with our Mustangs, and pilot talk was universal, demanding scarce translation. A young Russian pilot from Moscow even showed us a photo of his girlfriend he had mounted on his P–40 instrument panel. But, none of us would forget a well-endowed, young, blond female armorer carrying heavy belts of 50 caliber ammo slung over each shoulder. She winked at our Russian pilot as she began loading the machine gun rounds in his fighter's wings. Moscow girlfriend, watch out! Enemy forces abound!

As near as I could gather, the Kremencuc Airfield Command had been alerted by the Soviets to look out for us. I wondered how we escaped being fired at ... let alone rescued and welcomed onto their airfield.

The rains stopped and the sun shined intermittently. Our hosts set up an outdoor picnic with tablecloths, delicious sandwiches, salads, and fresh milk from Kremencuc cows. I hadn't tasted fresh, cold milk since leaving the states in May of 1943, and being a kid not yet weaned from cows, I savored the treat. As for the sandwiches, I didn't know nor care what they were. We were all famished and they hit the spot.

We had to resume our mission, so I asked the officer who met me at my plane (the P–40 squadron CO) for directions. He made signs and spoke in Russian, but seemed to say, "Poltava? Nothing to it." Then he laid a map on the picnic table and pointed out Poltava only 30 or 40 miles away. Ironically, an IRON BEAM went directly there.

With trepidation, we borrowed some gas back from Roosevelt's Russian Lend Lease. The Russians had only 90–octane and we were concerned whether it was rich enough for our Packard-Rolls prop drivers. We deliberated and decided to add only about twenty five gallons to each plane. We believed that such a minimal amount would not dilute our remaining 130–octane too much, but still get us there. Since I was lead plane, I had used less than the others and opted not to add any. We let our remaining 130–octane flow through the carburetors while warming up.

None of the engines significantly acted up during magneto checks on the ground nor on takeoff. Off we went again, this time pointing our noses down the infallible iron beam. I called on the designated channel and offered the prearranged code for the Poltava Air Base. Amazingly, I got a reply from the tower in English. I first requested Fry be cleared straight in because his engine was running rough. Eight hours after take off from Italy, the ten of us landed safely in Poltava. "You were saying, Prosecutor?"

Russian Hospitality Pot Lash

American maintenance crews met us and immediately began servicing our aircraft. It was an unexpected welcome, but for the first time, I considered the trip home. Surely, it wasn't a one-day boomerang trip? We needed some time for rest and interface with the ground crew. But I needn't worry. While in the process of learning that only my own and one P–38 squadron had arrived thus far, I counted ten Mustangs buzzing the field. They were just arriving from another auxiliary field located nearby. This sure looked encouraging until later I was thrashed by the news that thirteen Mustangs of the 2nd and 5th Squadrons were presumed down. Flak along the Russo-German front apparently hit two or three of the planes, but predominately, weather and navigational errors were the culprits. What an abominable outcome. We did eventually recover several pilots and planes among those that safely found other soviet airstrips or crash-landed in the wheat fields

We bedded down in tents, which I'm sure was part of a Russian hospitality program to keep us from getting homesick. Major Wiley was offered a room with a bed and sheets. He was one of the guys and so declined. We got together for a brief post-mortem with Major Fuller and some of the other mission survivors the following morning. The squadron leaders of both the P–38 and P–51 groups then reported for a debriefing. A bird colonel and two subordinates were seated at a long table covered with papers. I saluted even though I was sorely out of practice.

> The colonel addressed me, "You're 4th Squadron, McCampbell?" "Yes Sir," I proudly answered.
>
> The colonel continued, "I'm sorry ... Is that Major McCampbell?"
>
> "No Sir."
>
> He lifts his pen, "Ah, Captain McCampbell"
>
> "No Sir, I'm Lieutenant McCampbell."
>
> "We need the 4th Squadron Leader," said the colonel. "I'm sorry."
>
> "Me too, Sir. But I am the assigned squadron leader."
>
> The colonel cleared his throat and stammered. "Oh, ahh fine."

He then interrogated me about the mission. This rank insult was followed by a discussion with the other squadron leaders, all of whom out ranked me. They agreed that the mission had been a mess due to weather compounded by inadequate preparation.

Political Discussions, Nyet!

On our second and last night in the USSR, a Russki squadron leader invited me to dinner. He spoke decent English and drove me in another U.S. Jeep to a local restaurant. The place was tolerable but not the Ritz. Both sexes were represented in the clientele, but were predominantly soldiers in uniform. He asked if I liked "woadka." How could I say no? When in Russia ... The vodka was served in old fashioned, eight-ounce café barrel-glasses. My host hoisted glass and toasted America. In turn, I toasted the Soviet Union. He must have noticed me wince when I drank my first mouthful of undiluted Russian vodka. If we could only have had some of it to add to our gas tanks in Kremencuc!

USSR run of August 1944
Author in first row center
Photo courtesy of Bob McCampbell

We had a tough steak. But to someone who had been steakless for over a year, it was delicious. The dinner conversation was favorable as well. I recalled the lone admonition from the Group Intelligence Officer ... "Don't get into any political discussions with the Russians!"

So, throughout the evening what did we do? We talked about our respective leaders and political systems. By the time my host ordered another glass of vodka I doubt if we knew what the topic was anyway. But we were both smiling and happy as he dumped me back at my tent.

Ambushed a Second Time?

The remainder of our squadron staggered back to the tent farm some time later and woke me with an awful rendition of a Russian drinking song. They were wearing Soviet airmen's caps, insignias, and other adornments, and had traded away many of their own. We were scheduled to check our planes out and be off for the return trip by early morning. After a cursory exam, I diagnosed their condition as worse than their singing. The new morn arrived too fast. The prevailing Poltava powers allowed me a stay of a few hours to give our poor flyboys time for the Alka-Seltzer to work.

Even though the squadron malaise seemed to exceed the powers of the antidote, I decided at about 1100 hours it was high time for our return takeoff. The skies were clear and the forecast was for more of the same.

Prior to departure we received a short briefing by American officers at Poltava which restated our return trip mission objective. It was even more indefinite that the one that got us here. This time we were tasked to hit "targets of opportunity".

I felt we'd already been one thanks to our Russian welcome.

Fighter Pilot's Dream

Of more sobering interest to us was an astonishing report of the exploits a previous Mustang shuttle mission. It seems that the 31st Fighter Group, a nearby Italy-based neighbor of ours, made a couple of fighter sweeps out of Poltava. One such mission the Mustangs of the 31st surprised an unescorted enemy force of about 40 Stuka Ju87 dive bombers. These deadly accurate, but obsolete and woefully vulnerable aircraft, were poised to strike a large Russian tank column. The Russian tanks would have been particularly at the mercy of the Stuka's newly mounted 40 mm anti-tank wing cannons. But not to worry Yuri! Many of the American Mustangs ran out of ammunition while destroying at least 30 Stukas without the loss of a single Mustang. The few surviving Stukas, if they returned to their bases at all, must have done so carrying a contagious morale problem.

With a unanimous affirmative vote from a quick impromptu meeting amongst our guys, I got an official OK to include about an hour's search for enemy aircraft along the front as a return trip priority.

As we gained desired altitude and neared the Russo-German front, I could feel it. Even though they harbored hangover handicaps, the guys had found a magic elixir. We were all so inspired by the 31st pilots' reality experience in nurturing the dream of every fighter pilot ... and to think the dream had been realized in the air space we were about to enter.

We had decided to cruise at 15,000 feet over the front, zigzagging a course of about 100 miles. But, after a disappointing neck and eye stretching exercise revealing nothing but a few low-flying Russian airplanes, and high-enemy flak bursts, it was time to head for our Italian pasture ... a mere 1,000 miles away. As a poor compromise we later spotted a rare daring daylight freight train chugging through western Rumania. Wile I stayed above for top cover with the other three guys of Tackle Red Flight, I sent Bullock and the remaining six Mustangs in a quick attack. With a couple of passes each they derailed and pretty well demolished the train.

Shepherds Guide Their Flocks

Resuming the journey home we were soon nearing the radius limits (about a 150 miles) of our friendly radar navigational aid station. They could triangulate our exact location from their three radar stations and orally give us our distance and direct compass headings to Madna from where ever we were. The station would regularly update us with corrected headings for the shortest distance home. The system saved many an airman's life who was returning short of fuel or long on other problems. Too bad our stations didn't lure a few enemy airplanes astray with that capability. As a matter of fact, the enemy did set up such a snare attempting to misdirect us. The project was so ill-scripted and poorly acted that the plot was clearly obvious and became a joke among Allied pilots.

Bad News ... Good News

As we welcomed the sights and communications from our home base at Madna we were soon happily on the turf, basking in the welcoming shouts and high jinx of joy from our individual ground crews.

I hadn't realized the extent of the 52nd's losses on the USSR trip until the debriefing during the late afternoon of our return. As you will recall, my 4th

Bob and his WD-D, home from the USSR
Photo courtesy of Bob McCampbell

Squadron had lost one, Stewart, from the initial and only enemy aerial encounter of the mission. The 2nd and the 5th Squadrons had lost seven more from flak and weather. Two of their pilots were being returned by the Russians. The P–38s had lost five; one pilot being returned in a dramatic rescue by a squadron-mate.

My Own Railroad Tracks

Tim Tyler returned the next day. He congratulated me saying, "Damned you Mac, you took my squadron! And you know if you hadn't used it to run off all those enemy airplanes in my place I might have been a hero. Wiley tells me you did a hell of a job from start to finish. He says if the 4th Squadron hadn't sent those Huns home with their tails between their whatever, they could'a caught the 38s like sittin' ducks on the deck." Tyler stood me at attention and pinned a pair of railroad tracks (captains bars) on my shirt.

My God, finally, I mumbled to myself. I knew he was thinking the same since he had initiated Tribbett's and my promotions to the point of frustration. Tyler then confided he was submitting my name for a Silver Star, citing my actions on the Russian mission in protecting the P–38s. I felt I had done little to earn that level of award. Still, I was euphoric! I had completely forgotten about the missing map section and all the other hairy events of the previous few days. Anyone could see that the "Prosecutor's sword had been broken over the General's knee."

Russian Mission Story - September 3, 1944
Courtesy of Santa Barbara News Press

Honors Crowd Action In McCampbell's Log

15TH AIR FORCE IN ITALY—The turnover from July to August was an important event to Lieutenant Robert H. McCampbell, 21-year-old P-51 Mustang pilot from Santa Barbara. On the last day of July he was presented the Distinguished Flying Cross and within a matter of days he flew a shuttle mission to an American base in Russia, bagging his third enemy plane in a thrilling fight on the way there.

The citation accompanying the D.F.C. award reads, in part: "Lieutenant McCampbell led his flight as escort to heavy bombers on a mission against strategic enemy installations in Romania. Enroute to and from the target large formations of enemy fighters persistently attempted to penetrate the fighter cover to attack and break up the bomber formation. Despite the superiority in numbers of enemy aircraft, displaying outstanding leadership, courage and combat skill, Lieutenant McCampbell so effectively disposed his formation that all attacks were successfully repulsed, thus enabling the bomber formation to complete a highly successful mission unmolested."

ROBERT McCAMPBELL

...G 7 NAZIS

During the fight, his formation shot down seven of the enemy would-be aggressors, Lieutenant McCampbell downing one with his own guns while directing the attack of his fellow pilots.

Close on the heels of the presentation, he was included in a mission shuttling to another American base in Russia, and through bad weather, heavy flak and difficult navigation, he not only completed his mission but when his formation was jumped by a large group of Nazi fighters, he shot down a Jerry that was attacking one of his fellow fliers.

"We were flying through a couple of layers of clouds when the Jerries came at us out of the top layer. It was a complete surprise, but they made only one pass and most of them split-essed for the deck. I pulled after one and sent a long burst into his fuselage and got his engine," was all the flier had to say of the battle. He was leading his squadron on the mission.

NEW VERSION TOLD

But Major James R. Wiley of Ocala, Fla., had a different story of the action. "Those Krauts surprised us all right," he said, "and one of them was hot on my tail, trying to fix it so I'd never get to Russia. Mac changed the situation in a hurry, and it was the Kraut that never got to where he was going."

Back from Russia, the Santa Barbara flier had two things to say about the Russians. "I heartily approve of them as allies—they're a great bunch of fellows." But later he added, "They missed me, though, on the Vodka business. They told me it was just like wine, and I had to find out differently for myself."

IN TOUGH GROUP

With a total of three aerial victories, Lieutenant McCampbell has completed more than a year of overseas duty and has been awarded the Air Medal with six clusters. His group recently completed two years of overseas service as a unit and has more than 360 enemy planes destroyed to its credit in addition to its many conquests in dive-bombing, strafing, and almost every type mission deemed possible for the fighter airplane.

McCampbell's mother, Mrs. Eula McCampbell, resides at 821 West Valerio street and his wife, Josephine, lives at 1759 Prospect avenue in Santa Barbara. His father, Lloyd E. McCampbell, assigned as a second lieutenant with the artillery during World War I, is a resident of Ventura.

Chapter 13

Regards to Broadway and Home

Déjà Vue All Over Again

I flew five more missions in August 1944. In mid-month an army of American, British and French forces invaded the Mediterranean coast of Southern France. I was assigned to lead the squadron as we provided fighter protection for the invasion forces. P–47 Thunderbolt fighters were doing the dirty work of close air support for the troops. Dive-bombing, strafing and dodging flak were their games. We were to beat off any enemy air opposition at a higher altitude. On this mission, Colonel Levine suggested he would like me to lead the squadron as assigned and he would lead one of its four-plane flights. I suggested, "Please Colonel, You do the squadron leader spot, sir, I'll take one of the flights." "No Mac, I've only flown a few missions since North Africa. I would prefer to follow your lead this time and to get me up to speed for the next trip."

Levine had led our 4th Squadron air offensive through the North African campaign. In that relatively short but heavily contested battle for air supremacy, the American Spitfire squadrons had then uniquely garnered more victories than losses. The U.S. subsequently produced not only superior fighter planes, but filled them with more experienced pilots. But in the North African on-the-job training war, the U.S. pilots were grateful to fly Spitfires and to be led by people like Bob Levine. He had been only 24 years old when he took over our 52nd Fighter Group in fall of 1943. The new Army Air Force had pressured him to stay for a career at war's end. This was a time when the military was dumping most of the rest of us. Bob, an exceptional wartime leader, had other ideas. He was to become in civilian life an accomplished attorney and later a highly respected pediatrician. He certainly should have been featured in Tom Browkaw's recent best seller *The Greatest Generation.*

On this mission we evaded occasional enemy flak by staying high above the invasion forces and merely bored holes in the sky while unsuccessfully searching for enemy planes. We could have been more helpful lending support to the P–47 Thunderbolts in their more direct support of the ground forces, but clearly, we couldn't abandon our job of high cover. The French resistance people had been harassing the German

P – 47 Thunderbolt
Photo courtesy of www.warbirdalley.com

forces from the rear and targeting would have been tough. Upon our return, Levine surprised me with the news that he, Bullock, Tribbett and I were being ordered stateside in early September ... *Wow!*

As we lazily followed our zig-zag course, sheep-doging our flock of B–24s, I dwelled on selfish things. It was September 1, 1944, my last 4th Squadron mission, supposedly. There were ever fewer enemy fighters in the skies ... still anti-aircraft fire but, if my good old Rolls Royce would keep churning I should beat the odds with a return ticket to Santa Barbara ... Yep! There are still occasional calls wafting the airways with reports of unidentified enemy aircraft. If enemy they were, they're likely looking for unescorted bombers and that would be unlikely with our now ever-swelling supply of fighters and pilots.

> *Another milk-run? Must be a time for me to unwind in reverent afterglow. As for the enemy ... a real foreboding. Hitler was still throwing parties but his own vaulted, tired and diminishing Luftwaffe was failing to RSVP.*

I asked the squadron to pull the formation in tight as we buzzed the Madna airstrip. I chopped the throttle, pulled up vertically and dropped full flaps to complete the tight landing circle. My wingman stayed in close formation all the way to touchdown.

> *Sure will miss my buddies staying behind, especially McCauley. God, for those whose return tickets may never arrive, my most solemn prayers are with you and your loved ones ... I know we'll meet again. Why was I so lucky?*

In respect to, but not in answer to this question, here's one for the record. Of the original five, Bullock, Gross, McCauley, Tribbett and me, "hired" by the 4th Squadron in mid-July 1943, Gross was missing in action and the only one lost to flying. In dramatic contrast, 16 of those 20 Spitfire pilots in the 4th were lost during the 3½ months of combat out of Calvi.

Treading Water Toward Home

As you may recall, we had been moved overseas by air ... Not exactly first class, mind you, but traveling that far by air, in those days, carried some prestige. Of course, that was when we were higher priority cannon fodder. Our trip home as spent cartridges carried considerable less prestige. It was there I learned that the term, "RHIP" (rank has its privileges), was reserved for field grade officers (majors and above). Captains and below did retain the privilege given all officers, that of paying for their own uniforms.

We were herded aboard ship at Naples harbor sometime in September 1944. This large freighter was a rust bucket that had traded hands between the French and the Germans several times since the outbreak of WWI and mid WWII. It had never been a real luxury liner. It was crewed by the French and its flag spoke the same language. It was to be a long voyage home from Naples, more than a fortnight. Trib was assigned to some kind of troop management duties and was thereby billeted in a suite on the upper deck of the type reserved for field grade officers. In contrast ordinary Army captains (like me) and below, were stowed away in large crowded, narrow passenger holds with triple deck bunks and chow lines. Many of the officers and enlisted traveling in this steerage class were returning U.S. air crew prisoners of war evacuated from Italy and the Balkans. Many were apparently not in the best of health. It seemed to me the country could have provided better for these guys.

It didn't take but a matter of minutes to determine that the only place to be in this environment was out on deck. September on the Mediterranean, and the Atlantic, was temperate. Comfortable seating was scarce but it was good to get some exercise. Maybe towards midnight the on deck crowd would thin out enough to permit a little jogging. God, this would be a slow trip to anywhere … especially home.

A Guitar Beckons

As I strolled the deck I heard a sound that was music to my ears. Actually it was the sound of live music coming from a young Lieutenant and his guitar. He was strumming and singing popular and folk songs. A few of the pilgrims were sitting around him joining in. I stopped and joined the joining in.

The strummer, it happened, hailed from Piru, California, a small slightly inland ranching community between Santa Barbara and Los Angeles. This had to be a rare circumstance. I had only once in the last 20 months crossed paths with anyone from or nearby my hometown, Santa Barbara. Santa Barbara's population was then about 30,000 and Piru's a scant 400, if you counted the few ranch people shopping at its general store.

The strummer was a Piru rancher's son. In my growing up years I had known little about Piru. An aunt and uncle of my Dad's had owned and operated a small hotel/boarding house there. The cozy rooms once had majestically arisen out of greater downtown Piru as one of its largest building (two stories). The strummer and I happily reminisced about our respective kid times and he taught me a few guitar chords and launched me on a lifetime of musical pleasure.

Bumped Up to First Class

It seems to me we were only on our 2nd or 3rd day of the cruise and who do you suppose lowers himself to visit me down amongst the common folk? ... None other than Tribbett, my old squadron mate and more recently an RHIP person himself. Before I can frame my envy-tainted greeting, Trib offers, "Hey Mac! Got a great job for you." I asked whether it was firing the boilers or swabbing the deck or another surprise trip to Russia? "Mac!" he says, "Got you on the O.D. (Officer of the Day) duty list. Get your stuff. You'll be billeted in my stateroom."

What a contrast from my initial shipboard accommodations. The stateroom was relatively spacious with three luxury double deck bunks, and a private bath. It housed six of us special-duty captains in the luxury accorded higher-ranking officers. We were also served in their dining room, which provided linen table cloths and napkins and real china. Waiters offered delicious French cuisine including killer pastries. Can't remember my duties too well but they were not too onerous or challenging. What I remember most was the un-crowded upper deck sunbathing, jogging and relaxing in a deck chair with a book ... and, of course, gorging on that gourmet food. Tribbett, my travel agent, had transformed my voyage into a posh ocean cruise. After all, he did owe me a favor for taking his Russki trip.

The cruise was still long and didn't leave the war completely behind. We were a part of a large convoy. The danger of submarine attack was omnipresent and boat drills occurred daily without warning. A Navy Corvette continued to escort us along side and in heavy seas seemed to play submarine itself. Fortunately the drills all turned out to be practice ones.

Sober Thoughts

The day finally arrived when the New York skyline appeared, soon to be followed by the Statue of Liberty. It may seem trite but the old girl gave me goose bumps and a feeling of sober reverence. I guess the reverence was really focused on all my revered young buddies who would not be coming home like I was.

We were warned on boarding to expect a strict customs inspection upon arrival. We had been admonished that any attempt to bring in firearms or ammunition would carry serious penalties. I had given up several such souvenirs prior to departure. But I couldn't bring myself to part with my little Italian Beretta automatic pistol. I had toted the Beretta in my right leather jacket pocket on each of my eighty visits over enemy skies. The Army in Europe had issued us Colt 45 automatics that were so heavy and cumbersome, I had opted for the Beretta. It had become such a natural accessory it was comparable to the feel of a wallet in my hip pocket. Hence, I walked down the gangplank and through customs with trepidation ...

but no strip search! I still cherish the Beretta but I've had no desire to carry it since, or any lethal weapon.

I believe the name of the Army camp where we were lodged outside of New York City was Fort Mead. We were only to be there for a couple of days while transportation for home-leave was arranged. We were ordered not to leave the camp for any reason. Upon hearing these words, Trib and I looked at one another like kids being told; "Don't put beans in your ears." With a single mind, we decided that it would be cruel and in-human punishment to deny two

Give our regards to Broadway!
Tribbett, the author and friend
Photo courtesy of Bob McCampbell

war-weary soldiers a night on the town, especially New York town. Another Air Force captain joined us and we had no trouble at the gate gaining our freedom. From there we cabbed into Manhattan and systemati-cally began hitting the nightclubs of fame. The Coco Cabana and Jack Dempsey's are a couple I remem-ber well. We wound up at the Roseland Ballroom and danced with some New York accented girls till the wee hours. We escorted them home to mother and were back under military care just before sunrise.

Back On The Iron Beam

At least the Army was consistent in its travel arrangements. You may recall I was rushed overseas from California, priority air. Now after bobbing along on the Atlantic for almost three weeks on a creaky scow, I am now offered a transcontinental dash home on a series of slow troop-weary cattle cars. Can't remember how long that took, but the entire trip from Naples home had to have been arranged by a non-flying Army officer.

Most things about homecoming were naturally heartwarming. Not too many contemporary male friends around, of course. My Mom, who never thought I would return, was as overjoyed as any warring son's mother could be. My then wife, Jo, and I were mutually moved by the occasion. We did however, need some degree of reacquainting after nearly a year and a half. My Dad in Ventura couldn't wait to show me off to friends, his refinery employees and the Lions Club. My wonderful in-laws, likewise, flattered me by inviting friends in for social gatherings.

Rest and Reassignment

A short stay at home and Jo and I were off to an Army occupied R&R hotel/spa in Santa Monica. Following about a week of top entertainment by Hollywood stars staged at the hotel, I was assigned as an instructor for a fighter training squadron based in De Ridder, Louisiana. While lounging at the spa, I was given a flight physical and did I get a surprise. Upon studying one of my x-rays an Army doctor questioned, "When did you fracture your upper back?" I swallowed and groped for an answer since at the time I was aiming for a regular commission and a career in the Air Force. "Had an accident, it's absolutely no problem now." What a lie! Following any heavy lifting or jarring, exercise I was experiencing extended periods of both upper and lower back discomfort.

Chapter 14

Top Secret and Shanghaied

Slave Quarters Hospitality—October, 1944

I bought a 1936 Buick Century coupe from Jo's dad. It was a straight eight, in excellent shape and built like a tank. It cruised beautifully down into the Deep South where hospitality spreads itself like southern drawl — well sorta.

This was late October 1944 and the only available hotel in De Ridder, Louisiana was dirty and infested with bed bugs and cockroaches. De Ridder is a town of less than 10,000 people, located about 25 miles east of the Texas border and 75 miles north of the Gulf of Mexico. The only other place we could find to rent was a barely furnished shack on a farm, with an outdoor porch out-house and no hot water. To give it some class it was offered at a Beverly Hills price. I doubt that such inhospitality would pass southern rental code minimums today. Gratefully, in two weeks, we got into a bare-bones, relatively modern housing project with an indoor toilet and bathtub.

The good news was the squadron came equipped with the latest P–40s, the P–40N. The bad news was the latest wasn't a whole lot of improvement over the first ones. In the early months of the war the P–40 was a foot-in-the-door fighter, better known as the plane of the renowned Flying Tigers. A few brave and innovative American pilots flying P–40s, and even P–39s, held off superior enemy air forces until more and better American planes were developed and pro-

Curtiss P – 40
Photo courtesy of www.warbirdsalley.com

duced. But by the close of 1943, flying P–40s against the Luftwaffe's best fighters was becoming duty above and beyond the call.

As I gazed on the row of P–40s lounging along the flight line on De Ridder Army Air Base, my thoughts rewound,

> *It was late September 1942, Luke Field Arizona and the hot desert sun was setting on my last day as an aviation cadet. Jim McCauley and I were hanging around the line to watch trainee pilots from the Republic of China go through some final flying exercises. They were flying P–40's and we were envious. All we had ever flown were trainers. These were real fighters.*
>
> *We turned to walk away but heard the sounds of unfamiliar engines. We jerked our heads around and watched in amazement as two unidentifiable fighter planes buzzed the runway and peeled up and around the flight pattern at*

speeds we had never before seen. We ran down the line as they landed and they taxied over to parking spots for transient aircraft. As the lead pilot jumped down from his plane, McCauley got in a word while a small crowd gathered.

"Man! What a plane you got there!"

"You can say that again," the pilot responds.

"Where do we go to get assigned to these?" McCauley asks

"England ... Try the RAF"

"What are these anyway?" continues McCauley.

Turns out the planes were being built for and ferried to Great Britain by North American Aviation, Inglewood California. RAF roundel insignia and camouflage decorated the aircraft. The U.S. Army didn't seem to have much interest in the "Mustang."

I mention this memory to document the likelihood that this, the Mustang, could have been available to the Army Air Corps a year sooner (Fall 1942 rather than Fall 1943). Even so, the Mustang contributed more than any other fighter to the demise of the Luftwaffe.

When I arrived for duty at De Ridder, the trainees in my new outfit were commissioned officers who had completed flight school and had gained reasonably competent flying skills. What I believed they lacked in the basic training program was an practice on techniques most effective for long-range fighter escort duties. I was confident that I had absorbed battle-tested doctrines on fuel management, tactics, intercepts, bomber rendezvous and protection, especially as practiced and endured in long-range, high-altitude situations. As a trainer, I believed I could be an asset to these young pilots.

There were some problems. For example, practicing intercepts was difficult. A–36 light bomber squadrons were available for such exercises but the bombers were too speedy for the P–40s to catch.

Note: Sometime in 1942 the USAAF bought 500 aircraft fitted with dive brakes and underwing weapons pylons. These were initially designated the A-36A Apache, but later retained the name Mustang. Other versions of the Mustang were built as reconnaissance aircraft and designated F–6A through F–6K.

Even fighter tactics training was limited somewhat due to the P–40's limited altitude and general performance. Again, aerial gunnery didn't seem to be an especially high priority. Still, I was able to institute training on some of the more obvious needs relating to my experiences. The trainee pilots and I got along well but I can't say the same for how I handled my relationship with my squadron CO. It was the only real interpersonal clash I left unreconciled during my military tenure.

Part of our training objective was to hone our nighttime strafing skills toward certain Japanese home island targets. I couldn't imagine a more unsuitable airplane than the old P–40 for this job. The P–40 was even unsuitable and unsafe to practice such a mission in. There were any number of available aircraft, which could be used much more effectively. Since the P–40 inventory was in excess of any foreseeable need, perhaps someone was proposing this training program as an "expediential aircraft disposal program."

At any rate, my preferred training agenda was ordered to the back burner. Guess I needed to apply for a job in the war again. Double-trouble was that my very positive performance rating and career recommendations, which Major Tim Tyler had kindly added to my personnel jacket had strangely vanished.

In February of 1945, the squadron was moved to Stuttgart, Arkansas. It had been a cold winter in the south but by early spring Stuttgart was starting to bust out all over. Housing wasn't a lot better but a bunch of the marrieds were beginning to find some recreation besides elbow bending in the Officer's Club. We began playing tennis on the public clay courts offered by the city of Stuttgart. My back was reminding me of a broken Spitfire, but it was so much fun hitting balls again, the ache was becoming secondary.

Telephonus Interruptus

I had no sooner began relaxing over early evening dinners at home, still in my tennis shorts, when the phone jingled and a duty officer relayed,

"Captain McCampbell?"

"Speaking"

"We have received some urgent orders for you. They direct you to report to a new duty station departing by military air at 2000 hours."

This was incredulous. *Must have been one of my old squadron buddies with a practical joke.* I replied that such a sudden duty change would be impossible. After all I was living off base with my wife, my car and other personal items and encumbrances.

"Don't the orders state to where or what duty I'm reporting?"

The duty officer answered in the negative and only offered that the orders were Top Secret. I added that I would be there to discuss the matter with someone in authority within 30 minutes.

"Captain, my advice is to pack your bags and have them with you when you arrive for the discussion."

Understandably, my wife was in a panic, I was in a panic, and it was nearing 1830 hours!

Chapter 15

AWOL with a Stolen Plane

Leaving On a Fast Plane

The duty officer was right about two things. First, he did have top secret orders specifically placing me on an awaiting airplane. Two, there was no one in authority available to discuss the matter. Our training squadron had been temporarily assigned to the base and my CO had been on leave. I was even unable to contact anyone in authority at our next echelon headquarters. A B–25 bomber was ready to load with engines idling. With concerns, reluctance and disbelief I climbed aboard.

The only bright spot on this confounding mystery sat beside me in a makeshift seat. There, buckling up was another captain, one Jim Felix, who was a recent addition to the small group of fighter pilot instructors in our squadron. Since he was not one of the marrieds, we had become only slightly acquainted. Felix was furious. He was a tough little five by five guy; a RAF transfer to the U.S. Army Air Corps who had flown P–40s for the British 8th Army in the western desert. Naturally I couldn't quite empathize with his problems as I measured them against mine. But obviously he had some and he wasn't going to take this freaking Army stupidity lying down, especially in the aft of an old B–25.

We were flown to Alexandria Army Air Base, Louisiana, only about 250 miles south. No one in headquarters nor operations there could direct us ei-

ther. We had figured we must be boarding something
bigger toward the Pacific. After a few drinks at the
Officer's Club we shrugged our shoulders, checked
into the BOQ, and slept in the next day. I had called
my wife and violated top secret orders provisions by
telling her I was not too far away, and would get everything straightened out in a couple of days.

The High Jacking

Around midday we finally located our first reporting place, there on Alexandria Air Base. A lieutenant running the office told us that the CO, Major
Carter, would have to brief us. The major was away
in Washington, DC and was expected to return the
following day. But, he didn't. Felix determined it was
time to take measures into our own hands. He reit-
erated that obligatory matters awaited him back in
Stuttgart, he would get us an airplane, we could fly
back up and take care of our personal things. He
would bring the plane back and I could return in my
car (easy for him to say) And Felix wasn't kidding. The
base operations officer authorized us to use an old
basic trainer, BT–13, for an instrument proficiency
training flight. "Local area only" was the prescribed
flying limit for our training. Felix obtained permission
to broaden this prescription, somewhat. We were allowed to navigate among several check point towns
covering a wider than local area.

The weather was appropriate for instrument
flying. It had been raining for days. Not only that, but
with the melting of the winter stuff, the Midwest was
awash, including an over-the-banks Mississippi. Felix
said he would navigate while I flew from the front seat.
As we soared into the wild gray yonder, I pondered the
consequences of what we were doing. Was the prosecutor going to take the stand again in my courts martial? The weather also reminded me of the Russia trip,

but we weren't about to climb up over the weather in this clunker.

I focused on my personal matters but Felix interrupted to give me an adjusted heading. We carried on a running conversation during the first part of the trip but soon I had to initiate each intercom. After about a 10 minute silence, with the weather deteriorating, I questioned our position and heading but got no answer in the intercom. I looked over my shoulder and Felix was snoring.

How Many Déjà Vues to a Customer?

Unbelievable! Here I was flying low, in bad weather again and with no map. The map and Felix were in the rear cockpit and both were useless. I tried some semi-aggressive maneuvers to awaken Felix but they were useless as well. The stormy weather had given us such a bumpy, uncomfortable ride I should have known further stick and rudder efforts would add little toward a wake-up call.

From all my P–40 trips around the area I should eventually find a familiar landmark. The rain and flooding were no help but after two hours flying in generally the right direction, a few towns and water towers stirred my memory. As a matter of fact I soon found myself directly over a long familiar trestle running toward Memphis about 20 miles northeast of Stuttgart. I immediately made a sharp U and the faithful iron beam choo-chooed me home. Felix had enjoyed a nip or two as well as a nap.

Top Secret Mystery Unravels

The next day, Jo and I crammed our belongings into the '36 Buick coupe and hit the long, wet, marginally navigable highways for Alexandria. What a mad, non-stop, 300-plus mile, southern odyssey that became. Major Carter returned to Alexandria on the same evening we arrived about midnight by car. Earlier that day, Felix had made it back with the BT–13. He had notified Alexandria base operations the day before when we had first landed in Stuttgart. Felix had relayed some cock and bull story about our getting lost in the storm and how we would be remaining overnight while a mechanic checked out a rough engine. I guess feigned gullibility sometimes saves as much grief for the story recipient as it saves for the prevaricator. Whew!

The next day Major Carter explained to us that our outfit was the 161st Liaison Group, and that our top secret mission was to perform certain defensive and support functions as a part of a task force. This task force was being formed to counter an aerial invasion of armed, unmanned Japanese balloons. He further explained that Felix and I and other officers would head up squadrons of light liaison planes working out of the Pacific Northwest. The whole thing seemed a peculiar wartime military undertaking to hold so close to the vest. Far as I was concerned the Japanese knew they were doing it. We knew they were doing it. Wouldn't the American public, alone in the dark, become more vulnerable and a wasted resource?

Smuggling the Big Secret Into the Northwest

After all the urgency and mystery of my original appointment to this new duty, the final idiocy of it all was summarized on a welcome note. Carter allowed me to drive my car and wife to Santa Barbara. The time of reporting necessitated a quick trip. Driving the Buick back home, I barely touched base in Santa Barbara and I grabbed another DC–3 flight to our new headquarters, McCord Field, Tacoma, Washington.

We newly appointed squadron COs spent a few days at McCord with briefings by Major Carter and an introduction to L–5 flying. As a cast-off Mustang pilot I had the feeling I was being demoted to the bottom of the pilot hierarchy. First suffering the indignity of the demotion to flying an obsolete fighter, the P–40 and now it was down to a piece of lightly motorized canvas that could have been outrun by the Red Baron in 1917. Such personal reflections, however, shouldn't cloud the truth. The L–5 was an outstanding airplane in its capability to do the job it was created for. Even more, the compliment of sergeant pilots who had flown them in Europe and the Pacific had done so with valor. I was soon to become proud and happy to be their CO and the only officer in my assigned squadron.

Chapter 16

Me ... The Ol' Man?

Auf Wiedersehen Nazis

In early May 1945, the end of the war in Europe was joyously anticipated. The western Allies had recovered from the Battle of the Bulge, and were moving toward Berlin. The Russians from the east were completing the stranglehold on the once seemingly invincible Nazi war machine. In the Pacific, the noose was also tightening around the Japanese home islands. The B–29 Super Fortresses were laying waste to Japanese cities, but suicidal enemy fighting on Okinawa created heavy casualties on both sides. Japanese *kamikaze* (suicide) bombers were still inflicting unacceptable losses on U.S. naval forces. I never doubted that within a short time I would wind up in the Pacific Theater.

Up, Up and Away

But what was this balloon menace anyway? I can find few people, even among my contemporaries, who knew then or know today about the operation. It wound up being one of the best-kept secrets of the war. To me it was a serious problem but ridiculous as a secret one.

The menace was actually a Japanese reaction to the famous Doolittle raid on Tokyo, back in April 1942. While the raid did little material damage, the psychological effect on the Japanese was substantial.

It baffled them as to how the Americans got there and Japan agonized over how to retaliate.

Ultimately, the Japanese launched a reprisal in the form of a balloon offensive. Some 9,000 paper or rubberized silk balloons were launched during a six-month period across the Pacific to North America. They each carried an antipersonnel and an incendiary bomb and followed the high altitude winds of the jet stream for more than 6,000 miles to our west coast and beyond. The first operational launches occurred in late 1944. They touched down from Alaska to Mexico and traveled as far to our east as Michigan. Most were sighted or found in the Pacific northwest. One, however, was found on the Santa Clara River shore of the Tobias Ranch, only a few miles from my home in Ventura, California. It is estimated that at least one thousand balloons successfully made landfall in the U.S. About 285 have been found to date.

Our government reasoned that the secret classification was necessary to prevent civilian panic and to deny the enemy information on the success of the operation. Sadly, in the state of Washington in May 1945, a minister, his wife and five Sunday school children on a church picnic found one of the balloons and were killed when its high-explosive bomb detonated. Following this tragedy the project was declassified and publicized.

The balloon assault, while never amounting to a critical threat to the U.S., may have been responsible for a few major forest fires. Most balloons, however, landed during the wet winter months. When spring arrived, the jet stream did not cooperate as a navigator. Still, many feared that with the spring thaw some of the incendiaries already down in the forests might ignite. Apparently, the Japanese intended to incinerate the vast and vulnerable national forests of the Pacific northwest and, perhaps, to terrorize some U.S. cities. The possibility of major forest fires stemming from languishing incendiaries or high explosives kept the balloon menace fighters in business for two months after the Japanese surrender in August 1946. All told, U.S. fighters knocked down fewer than ten balloons in six months. The balloons were just too hard to locate or hit.

Clever Japanese

The balloons were clever Rube Goldberg devices. Usually made of paper, they were about 32 feet in diameter, hydrogen filled, and carried several ballast bags as well as their bombs. They were built mostly by Japanese school children. They were self-controlled by several self-contained, well-oriented barometric altimeters, and were transported by the prevailing upper winds. The altimeters were located along a fuse circling beneath the balloon. If the balloon rose too high it was subject to destruction through over-expansion. An altimeter showing excess altitude ignited a fuse that tripped a valve to release hydrogen. If the balloon dropped too low in the jet stream an altimeter would fire a fuse that would burn down and release a sandbag. As the balloon descended and neared its journey's end, an altimeter would activate the release of the incendiary. The anti-personnel bomb was set to detonate upon impact as the balloon finally landed.

An Instant Administrator

My assigned squadron had a compliment of sixteen L–5s, twenty sergeant pilots to fly them, and about thirty other enlisted, including mechanics and their assistants. A squadron office clerk, Corporal Windside, was to become my Sergeant Bilko.

Gowan Army Air Force Base, Boise Idaho, was my new working address. Other squadrons were based in Washington, Oregon, Montana and northern California. I caught a C–47 to Boise to meet with federal and state forestry people, and my counterpart, a captain in charge of an Army engineer ground contingent. In less than two days we cranked out a program of surveillance and fire assistance and set up some initial communication procedures. It was a hit or miss operation, but within a week we were doing a productive job of cooperative air search. I like to think it was on-the-job-training at its best.

McCampbell at Office Duty
Photo courtesy of Bob McCampbell

Administrative duty was new to me and I felt overwhelmed at first. My first chore at Gowen was to meet with the base CO, a bird colonel who had been briefed on my arrival and mission. Gowen was a large base with B–24 heavy bomber training as its primary function, yet the good colonel was more than helpful. He called a quick meeting of his immediate staff, advised them of the priority of my operation, and essentially gave me *carte blanche* in terms of his base resources. I even got a jeep. I hadn't felt so important since being commissioned a 2nd lieutenant in 1942.

Looking Over a Four-Leaf Clover

During the first few days I almost wore out the brakes, tires and clutch on the Jeep. I set up my office, got a flight ramp assigned for our airplanes and set up a small maintenance building on the line. I also got our men a barracks and continued to meet and confer with the forestry and Army engineer people.

The men and their L-5s, arrived from McCord Field, Tacoma, as I was still working on what to do with them. Couldn't have been luckier than to have acquired Master Sergeant Mack, our squadron NCO (non-commissioned officer). Mack was a strong, experienced, trustworthy leader and an excellent pilot. By the numbers he knew what had to be done and how to get it done.

Mack and the other pilots were decorated veterans of service ranging from Burma to the banks of the Rhine. They had flown generals around the battle fronts, and supplies, medicine, and medics into combat areas. They'd done combat observation missions and had regularly evacuated wounded out of almost irretrievable situations. I was learning to appreciate that people other than fighter pilots were also important to the war effort.

With all this support, most everything fell into place. In consort with the state and federal forestry people, we set up a system of surveillance using three-to-four L-5s patrolling out of four different remote locations. Our primary job was to spot balloon remnants or infant fires in the high mountains. We set up our pilots and crews in civilian or tent quarters at very small nonmilitary airstrips at Challis, Idaho northeast of Boise, at McCall, Idaho to the north and Baker, Oregon to the west. We also retained three L-5s patrolling out of our home base, Gowen Field. In this way we covered the more inaccessible segments of topography in our area of responsibility. We generally flew cloverleaf patrol patterns consistent with the L–5 range capacity.

Stinson L – 5 Sentinel
Photo courtesy of USAF Museum

I took over an L–5 from our flight at Gowen and spent a considerable amount of my time flying to the outlying strips to see how things were going and what was needed. I sometimes hauled supplies on such inspection trips. The flights, especially the round trips from Boise to Challis, were a little edgy. I had to get over 12,000 feet to clear one snow-bound mountain range. That is a long climb in an L–5. I felt somewhat at the mercy of the elements and seemed to stagger at that altitude in that little fabric-covered cocoon. Such experiences made me better appreciate what our L–5 guys were doing every day.

The Corporal Caper

Anti-balloon duty became quite satisfying. With the war almost over, there was only one fly left in my ointment ... Corporal Windside, my office clerk. He had arrived a few days after the other squadron men, and I thought my administrative and clerical problems were solved. Paperwork was a daily nuisance for which I'd had no particular interest, experience nor knowledge. Windside assured me he could handle all of it only bothering me for an occasional signature. I should have seen a problem developing here.

The first few days went well. My relationship with the men seemed excellent and the dreaded paperwork appeared under control. But, I should have recognized the warning signs as Windside incrementally pushed the limits of propriety. He was overbearingly complementary and patronizing, and had a running dialog of rhetorical questions. I can still hear him, "Captain, since I'm alone in the office much of the time and the only one cognizant of our administrative things ... and the only one to answer our phone ... and answer and take care of our men's questions and paperwork ... I'm really acting top sergeant, aren't I?" I would reply something seemingly innocuous like, "Well, I'm sure you are doing many of the things that might be required of some top sergeants ..."

One day Sergeant Mack dropped by to ask if I would look at something posted on the barracks bulletin board. I accompanied him into a building filled with angry men. Two separate administrative orders were posted outlining barracks duties and other responsibilities. The "salutation" on each was "By order of Captain Robert McCampbell," and signed by "Windside, Sergeant Major." They were not "my kind" of orders and were an insult to the dignity and intelligence, especially, of these combat-seasoned guys. I immediately pulled the "edicts" from the board and advised the men that Sergeant Mack was their non-commissioned officer in charge. I further advised that they were to disregard any posted orders unless signed by Sergeant Mack or myself. They cheered!

Windside even forged my signature on per diem pay orders covering himself and me under certain non qualifying travel conditions. The local finance officer allowed me to retrieve them without too much embarrassment. It struck me that my sternest admonishments were not enough. Never in my young life had I seriously admonished, punished or canned anyone. The aircraft crew chiefs and other flight maintenance guys in the fighter outfits were such dedicated, hard-working people, disciplinary situations were almost unheard of. I had killed a few people in combat, but that was different. This would be man-to-man verbal confrontation. I wasn't even sure how to go about it. Selfishly too, I didn't want to be left high and dry at this moment with the routine stuff that the guy was apparently handling in satisfactory manner.

In the middle of this deliberation, my headquarters at McCord sent me a great assistant of another kind, 2nd Lieutenant Jim Walls. He also brought a new airplane, a wife, and a two-year-old son. The airplane was a U.S. designated C–64, Noorduyn Norseman. It was of Canadian manufacture, a high wing, single-engine "bush plane" of about 600 horsepower. It had a duel cockpit and accommodated eight passengers and a copilot. We used the copilot seat for a ninth passenger seat if needed. Like the smaller L–5 it had deep flaps and could be landed on a dime. Otherwise, it was a large and cumbersome single engine brute. Some are still being used in Canada and Alaska, with and without floats, for passenger and freight hauls in the bush. Using it rather than the L–5 for visits and hauls between Gowen and my three outlying units became a most welcome advantage.

I even flew some top forestry officials over forest-fires to plan containment strategies. We flew to meetings at Yellowstone, and Jackson Hole Wyoming, and to their district headquarters, Ogden, Utah. We actually did a few parachuted equipment drops to fire crews with the C–64. Flying the beast didn't get you there very fast, but it sure got you in and out of some tight places. I was beginning to wonder if I shouldn't become an Alaskan bush pilot. But thoughts of warm

Me ... The Ole Man?

air and surf of my Southern California home wouldn't stop beckoning

In the meantime, Windside had crossed the line, to the extent that I no longer had any misgivings about what I had to do. An event occurred demanding immediate action on my part. I happened across him in a Boise restaurant one evening and found him flaunting master sergeant stripes and a clutter of unearned medals for bravery. He was partying in mixed company and I couldn't withhold confronting him on the spot.

To me, this behavior was an unforgivable insult to every military person who had ever earned battlefield honors. It constituted the ultimate disrespect to those who had given the full measure of devotion to their country; those who had earned the admiration of honors displayed on their uniforms but would never receive it. With Major Carter's concurrence, I removed the corporal from his duties the following day. He was sent packing to our headquarters with my charges against him wired ahead. With his replacement on the way, there was many a dry eye in the squadron.

Life's Hardly a Bore in the C - 64

With Jim Walls as a very level-headed backup squadron leader, the C–64 at my disposal, and my boss generously delegating my operations from afar, wartime duty could hardly get better. Likewise, my crews that were detached to the outlying non-military fields enjoyed a similar freedom from day to day military annoyances. I now paid them visits in the C–64. For the men at Challis, Idaho, our most remote outpost, my visits were special occasions. For them, I always brought some goodies as well as needed supplies.

I could haul a substantial load of supplies in that C–64. Once I got the thing to desired altitude, it was more reassuring traveling over the snowy 12,000 foot ridges in this big fellow than in an L–5. In a Mustang I hardly would have noticed those peaks.

Noorduyn Norseman C – 64
Photo courtesy of Noorduyn, Inc

In late July 1945, I flew the C–64 to a meeting at my McCord Field, Tacoma headquarters. There I discovered that my old buddy, McCauley, was the flight operations officer for McCord. We spent a couple days reminiscing over our wild wartime wanderings. It was heartwarming as well to see Jim's lovely wife Katherine. It had been a span of two years since I knew them as newlyweds in those Santa Rosa days. They obviously were weathering military life enviably well together.

Some days later I took the C–64 on a training flight home to Santa Barbara. This is about a nine-hour trip, including a fuel stop, in a 135 mph plane. As I approached home I called for landing instructions at the then vast Marine Air Station, Santa Barbara. My identification created some small confusion within the station's flight operations crew. The tower had asked for the rank of the senior officer present. The problem was that no one in the tower had ever heard of a C–64.

The Army Air Force "C" designation generally connoted a large commercial type aircraft, such as the four-engine C–54, which was then the largest of the AAF troop transports. Apparently, with that information, the Marines at hand figured the C–64 must be new and bigger and carrying some high rank. Of course, I responded to the control tower by radio that the senior rank aboard was captain. Now, while a captain wasn't an admiral or the president or such, the Marines did confuse my rank with that of a Navy captain. This would constitute rank equivalent to an Army or Marine Corps colonel.

It's possible they were still looking skyward for this new leviathan and its colonel when I slipped in and landed. The staff officer sent to meet me was bewildered, and after further communications between the tower and me, the staff car was recalled in favor of a Jeep. I snickered a bit, parked the ugly bird, and eventually caught a ride into town from a benevolent Marine. I could spend the weekend only, but friends and family were surprised and excited. My Mom was more relaxed than before. Apparently, she decided I might survive the war after all. I hoped she was right.

Balloon Payment

The return flight was more tedious but I collected a slight tail wind pushing my ground speed to an average of over 140 mph. Before setting out on course, I buzzed my Dad's refinery with the prop in low pitch and made almost enough noise to evacuate the majority of the Ventura Avenue homes and my Dad's refinery. The C–64 could draw attention.

On my return to Boise our top secret job still appeared to be going well. We hadn't found any balloons, but our guys had spotted some fledgling forest fires. This allowed the smoke jumpers to nip them in the bud. My sister squadron in Washington State had found a couple of the balloons down in the forests. But little else occurred considering our wide coverage of the skies and earth from mid-California north to Canada and east across Wyoming and Montana. Our small L–5 squadron and the Army ground troops were able to give considerable aid and logistics support to the undermanned county, state and federal fire fighting forces. I felt blessed that during my watch my guys had accomplished so many hazardous high mountain flight hours without a major mishap.

There you have it, a top secret that was declassified almost sixty years ago and today, it's still a best-kept secret.

Chapter 17

Farewell to Arms

Oops, We Uncorked the Genie

All along I believed that my mystery mission to the Pacific northwest would be only a side jaunt of the big trip to the Pacific. But it was not to be. The Japanese had ceased their balloon launches by early summer of 1945. The U.S. B–29 Superfortresses were beginning to gut major cities in Japan. The Japanese were running out of airplanes, ships and soldiers, as well as cities. Undoubtedly balloon production had tumbled down the list of Japanese priorities. The summer jet stream had even pooped out on its previously free ride to the states.

There is little historical doubt that some part of the Japanese government was dangling peace feelers by the beginning of August 1945. But, on August 6, 1945, an American B–29 bomber startled the world dropping a nuclear bomb on the city of Hiroshima. This action vaporized most of the large city and its dwellers. It was followed by another on Nagasaki on August 9, 1945. These awesome strokes amounted to the *coup de grace*. On August 10, the Japanese government formally agreed to an unconditional surrender. How the secret development of the atomic bomb was kept from the world, including most of us in the military, was almost as amazing a feat as the development itself. The controversy over the moral issue of our use of "The Bomb" continues. Only God could know the answer to that, as well as the consequences of man's unleashing of nuclear destructive power.

Out of a Job Again?

Accordingly, I was out of a job. Our balloon project was continued through September 1945 and I was loaded with administrative chores processing our men's requests for leave and movement to discharge centers. I obtained some really welcome help from the Red Cross, which aided with home leave problems and other family-related matters, especially for the lower paid men. I was sent to do the same shutdown job for one of our squadrons based in Fresno, California.

During this time I learned that I could remain in the service despite the forecast of massive military downsizing and demobilization. Since the airlines had advised me that they weren't interested in ex-fighter pilots, my service experience left me with few marketable skills. More worrisome was the fact I would soon be a 22-year-old father. But the final Catch-22 was that Jo insisted I not continue with military flying. I could understand her feelings. A number of my close friends and members of our social entourage were lost in flight training accidents on Jo's watch. Often they left behind grieving young wives. I reminded Jo that the frenzied pace of training and actual fighting would be not the norm, but my argument fell on deaf ears.

My cherished first-born, Nancy, arrived on October 28, 1945. After three weeks leave, and undergoing fatherhood training in Santa Barbara, I was ordered to Biggs Field, Alexandria, Louisiana, for reassignment. I went before a review board with my emotions about as mixed as they could get.

Should I make the Air Force a career? Should I get out? Couldn't the Army make the decision?

Well it did. I had tried some tennis while home and my back pain hadn't cooperated. The board clearly indicated I was to be retained on duty if I so desired. I indicated I would first like a medical review on my back injury before resuming new active duty. With no previous information about my injury the board scratched its head and sent me to the Barksdale Army Regional Hospital at Shreveport, Louisiana. Here I resided, mostly as an outpatient, until Christmas 1945. The treatment reminded me of my stay in the MASH unit in Corsica. This was my final military medical.

Eventually, after a few x-rays and knee raps, I was sent to a psychiatrist. Pardon the pun, but I was not too crazy about this. I soon realized he was there to facilitate my exit from the military in the least expensive manner. I had been caught malingering again. The shrink concluded that since my home was in southern California the warm climate would gradually cure me of whatever ailed my vertebrae.

Uh oh, this guy is trying to get me discharged without any record of a combat-related back injury.

I asked, "Didn't the medical review concur that I had suffered from a compression fracture?"

"Yes," he answered. "But it can't be concluded that it occurred as the result of military duty. It could have happened anytime in your adult life."

"But I have a Purple Heart for the injury!"

"Not specifically for a compression fracture, apparently some scalp and other lacerations," he added.

"But, I haven't had much adult life, except in the service."

It didn't matter. He was the doctor and he also out-ranked me. *Next case!*

The Fat Lady Sings

I was home for Christmas, and effective 31 January 1946, was honorably discharged (malingering or not) from the Army of the United States. It had been

four (*still mind boggling*) years earlier that I eagerly,
but apprehensively, departed home for Army Aviation
Flight Training. I was grateful that my life was spared
but forever distressed over those whose lives were
not. Again, *Why Me?* The French seventeenth century philosopher, Rene Descartes, in reconciling the
clash between the then emerging scientific evidence
and contradictory religious doctrine, pronounced in
effect, that " ... the mind of man was too infinitesimal
to comprehend the ways of the Lord." Amen to that!

Glory Limited to Fighter Jocks?

It was unbearably hard to say good-bye to my
days as a military fighter pilot. These had given me an
early hoist into a rarefied atmosphere of comradeship,
adult self-confidence and feeling of accomplishment. I
knew there were many who had done much more than
I, but, at least, I was a bona fide member of the club
... a very select club. I recently attended a Year 2003,
squadron reunion of those few pilots remaining of the
52nd Fighter Group's World War II warriors. There I got
a huge emotional fix that the Army psychiatrist could
never take away.

But before I get carried away about the select
club, what about the pilots and crews of other combat aircraft? What about those guys who carried the
heavy bomb loads for tortuously long missions to the
enemies' heartlands at, most likely, a greater risk than
ours? We were exhausted after five steady hours of escort flying. The bomber crews had to endure perhaps
twice that many flying hours from take-off, to forming
up, and to bomb run and back. The pilots laborious-
ly wrestled the controls of their cumbersome beasts,
while they and their crews, under miserably uncomfortable conditions, dodged enemy fighters and flak.
Moreover, the bomber pilot's unenviable situation left
him unable to do much defensively, and added greatly
to the stress overload of his world. His mandate was

to stay the bomber course, in formation, while the enemy's heavy anti-aircraft bursts were radar-directed to his altitude and while opposing fighters jockeyed for position.

And how about the troop carrier guys, who, in the night, brought in the paratroopers in at necessarily low, vulnerable altitudes. A large formation of paratrooper planes was mistakenly downed by the friendly fire of U.S. Navy ship-board gunners during the invasion of Sicily ... and the list goes on like the liaison pilots I'd known, who, with great skill and daring, flew their frail craft into jungle battlefield clearings to rescue downed soldiers.

The Battle of Germany

The air battle of Germany or roughly the war's last two years, employed the greatest numbers of planes and air crews ever assembled and undoubtedly far more than in any future war. So much more accuracy and damage can be inflicted today by one small fighter-bomber that target coverage by World War II standards would be redundant and bankrupting. There would hardly be sufficient production lead-time in any conceivable scenario.

Statistics on combat aircraft victories and losses in the battle of Germany are illusive and strangely enough, still debated. As a yardstick of magnitude, the Allies lost somewhere in the vicinity of 100,000 airmen in the battle. The American Army Air Forces alone lost over 18,000 aircraft. I recently visited the American Cemetery near Cambridge, England. There rest 30,000 American airmen whose names are honored on its massive, hallowed walls.

It could be argued that Germany won the battle for the skies by a 10-to-1 margin in terms of victories over losses, but they still lost the war. The devastation visited on Germany's war-making capability and its cities by Allied bombing left little more than a shell.

Among other things, the Germans figuratively and literally ran out of gas. They came close, early in the battle, to making our bomber losses so unacceptable that the raids couldn't continue. That didn't happen. The primary reason was the introduction, in late 1943 of the long range, high-performing American P–51 Mustang fighter. To the dismay of the Nazi leadership, and its pilots, the P–51 could not only tag along to any bomber target in Europe, but on the way and when it got there, spoil the Luftwaffe's previously extended heydays against our bombers.

The year 1944 saw the American fighter pilot pile up at least a 2-to-1 margin over Luftwaffe fighters. This is even more remarkable considering that predominantly the fighting was done deep over enemy territory. Further, the enemy pilots were increasingly prone to avoid confrontation with our fighters and seek out the preferred un-shepherded bombers.

By mid-year the elite corps of German aces was facing critical attrition. No other nation's pilots had amassed greater skills and successes in aerial combat than those of the Luftwaffe. A few had somehow survived well over a thousand missions. Talk about good on-the-job training! There were two Luftwaffe aces credited with more than 300 victories each. There were 34 others with 150 to 275 kills. Many of those most successful aces had been shot down, some over a dozen times and survived to return to a new cockpit. Still, no matter how proficient and formidable they were, hundreds of German aces were killed as they faced lady luck's inevitable law of averages and tougher opponents. It had been a risky business even for the greatest. The year 1944 heralded the last gasp of Germany's once-feared and mighty air arm.

Fighters that Changed World

Clearly, no fighter aircraft were more famous for their contributions to the demise of Nazi Germany than the Spitfire and the Mustang: the former for its role in stopping the invincible German war machine at the British shores in the Battle of Britain; the latter for subsequently wresting air superiority from the Luftwaffe in the farthest reaches of German skies. As a run-of-the-mill fighter pilot, I was damned lucky to fly both.

Perhaps an equally interesting but lesser known story relates the role the British government played in the development of the North American Mustang. Real aircraft buffs know that the Spitfire was designed by the famous British aeronautical engineer, R.J. Mitchell, who died in 1937, one year before the first production Spit was accepted by the RAF. Production problems were being overcome in 1940. But, far fewer Spits than Hawker Hurricane fighters were available by late summer, the start of the Battle of Britain. The Spits battled well, toe-to-toe with Germany's vaunted ME–109 fighters while the Hurricanes were better used against the German bombers. The rest of the battle story is well known. The RAF down to its last resources had dealt the Luftwaffe a loss rate considered by the Germans to be unsustainable. The battle was over. England was saved. On a recent trip to England (sixty-two years later) I noticed that if you just mentions the word Spitfire to a Brit, his or her eyes still light up!

In the winter of 1939-40, the British, desperate for fighters found the U.S in the early stages of lining up its available airplane production. Representatives of the British Air Purchasing Commission visited the relatively small North American Aviation Company requesting they tool up to produce some Curtiss P–40 fighters for the RAF. In April 1940, North American President Dutch Kindelberger advised that in his opinion the American fighters then in production would be hard-pressed to match the performance of the German fighters already in action over Europe. Kindelberger

and his staff offered and extolled the virtues of a preliminary design for a new, better fighter. He boasted
that he could do final design and build this higher
performing airplane within 120 days ... sooner than
he could tool up to produce P–40s. With incredibly
rapid negotiations incorporating additional engineering and design input, North American gained design
acceptance from the British. The contract named the
design Mustang and included their stipulation that
production of the experimental model indeed be completed within 120 days.

The exhaustive and innovative round-the-clock
effort by Kindelberger's dedicated workers and the resulting airplane are both legendary now. On the 100th
day, the experimental Mustang was out the factory
doors awaiting its hard-to-come-by Allison engine.
More frantic work occurred while the engine was mat-
ed to the Mustang airframe. But on the morning of 26
October 1940, test pilot Vance Breese taxied the first
Mustang out onto Mines Field runway. He pushed the
throttle resolutely forward, moving the Mustang down
and smartly off the runway for its initial test flight.
Breese, and subsequent American and RAF test pilots
all reveled in the plane's performance and beautiful
handling characteristics.

The RAF ordered 320 Mustangs and the first
of the production planes arrived in fall of 1941. The
RAF put them to work principally on low-level nuisance raids against various enemy ground targets.
The Mustangs more than lived up to expectation in
this job exploiting their speed in evading anti-aircraft
fire and enemy fighters. The U.S. ordered two of the
early production models for delivery to the Army Air
Force test facility at Wright Field, Ohio. Here they sat,
seemingly overlooked, for many months. It was during one of those months, December 1941, that the
U.S. was brought into World War II. It also happened
that in January 1942, while the two Mustangs were

still gathering dust at Wright Field, I was being accepted as a Flying Cadet in the U.S. Army Air Corps. The point of all this is, of course, that it's unlikely the P–51 Mustang would have ever been more than a discarded design concept if the Brits hadn't, as a last resort, called on Dutch Kindelberger in 1940 for some P–40s.

There was only one problem with the spunky P–51A Mustang. Its Allison engine didn't give it the needed rate of climb and performance at high altitude. Recognizing this limitation, the Brits in October 1942 began testing a modified Mustang driven by a Merlin Rolls Royce supercharged engine. The results beat expectations and the British licensed the American Packard Motor Co. to produce the Merlin XX engine for the Mustang. With some further design improvements by North American to better adapt the Packard Merlin, the new Mustang hurriedly was mass-produced with a performance and range superior to any other fighter anywhere at any altitude. You have to admit though, when you hear the unmistakable low melodious moan of that beautiful American fighter it does carry a heavy British accent.

How Did Spitfire and Mustang Compare?

Through the years, friends inevitably asked, "Which of the two fighters did you like the best?" In a way, that's akin to asking, "Did you prefer your mother or your wife?" Like the two airplanes, both were better to me than I deserved. Today a large color photo of an in-flight, RAF Spitfire Mark V reverently hangs in our family room (never could find a comparable snap of one with USAAF markings). Masquerading through the skies above the beautiful English summer countryside in its colorful camouflage and RAF roundel insignia markings is the ultimate in emotion-provoking artistry for me. My incessant nostalgia is generated partly from memories of piloting this incredible elliptical-winged wellspring of the Depression and partly from its role in crushing German efforts of conquest over that countryside.

Any comparison must consider that the development and early production runs of the Spitfire were taking place during the pre-war period when the science of aeronautical engineering was gaining remarkable momentum. But with the advent of World War II bringing its incentives and accompanying resources, the scientific breakthroughs, literally, went ballistic. So the Spitfire, as brilliant a design as it was, (and its production perfectly timed for the job it faced in 1940) didn't enjoy some of the developmental advantages gained by the later built Mustang ... Then again, no contemporary American fighter did either.

Both fighters went through many modifications through the war years, some of them involving major improvements. Accordingly I believe some meaningful and fair comparisons can be drawn from my experiences in flying the Spitfire Mark IX, a later Spit, versus those in the P–51B Mustang. These fighters were produced at roughly the same time during 1943 and I flew both. I should clarify that the Spits we flew on most combat missions, the Mark Vb, were essentially the same models as those used in the 1940 Battle of Britain. The most notable difference was the addition of two 20 mm wing cannon. The Spitfire Mark IX, we'll be using for the Mustang comparison incorporated the same British engine as the P–51B Mustang. This major improvement made the Mark IX clearly superior to our regular mission Spit Vbs.

But, all the Spit models I flew were pilot friendly in most respects. On my initial flights, in the older Spits, I marveled on take off at how much more comfortably it handled than the P–39 Airacobra, which I'd flown since cadet training. Instead of the mushy feeling of the P–39, until it got some speed, the Spit responded with solid stick and rudder control as soon as airborne. Diving and climbing in the Spit took some leg muscle, alternately on left and right rudder, but not to worry. Aerobatics were confidence building and the Spit was honest in stalls and spins. Spin recovery was easily handled with spin-opposing rudder and the stick popped forward ... almost as simple as with the old Stearman primary trainer. Best of all, while checking out in Spits at the North African training facility, we inevitably sought mock dog-fights against the other fighters based there. These were Lockheed P–38s, P–39 Airacobras, and Curtiss P–40s. We found we could easily turn inside all of them, which is a dogfight objective for getting on the other guy's tail. In fact, on one occasion, when a P–40's bout at low altitude with a Spitfire sadly resulted in the P–40's fatal spin-in, we were no longer allowed to engage them in dogfights.

I probably didn't fly the Mark IX on more than 10 flights. The two we had were kept on alert because of their high rate of climb and other performance advantages. But when they were flown, it was throttle to the wall to about 30,000 feet, commonly while attempting to intercept stripped down, high-speed, enemy photo reconnaissance planes. The Mark IX's climb rate (due to its lighter weight) was an astounding 4100 feet per minute, slightly faster from runway to 30,000 feet than the P–51B. The rudder controls, in accelerated climbs, were stiffer on the Spit without some bothersome attention to trim control. You had to stand on the opposite rudder as well in a dive. But, what a uniquely comfortable thrill following take off, to aim that Spit toward the moon and feel its seat back pushing firmly on your vertebrae.

At any altitude in level flight, the Mustang P–51B was faster, fetching a top speed of 440 mph at 30,000 feet. The Spit IX would do a very respectable 400 mph. Going downhill the Mustang really excelled, gaining momentum to the point where care had to be exercised at excessively fast diving speeds. The

Mustang could actually tease transonic speeds that sometimes confused its control surfaces. This condition necessitated some deceleration and a delicate pull out lest you leave the wings behind. It followed that the Mustang zoom (the speed and altitude thrust accumulated when pulling upward out a dive) exceeded that of the Spitfire. The obvious advantage, in this respect, was that the fighter getting the most out of the zoom wound up with the high ground.

The Spitfire could turn tighter than the Mustang, but the latter could get into the turn faster. As a matter of fact, just about everything you did with a Mustang was a bit easier to do. With its widely separated landing gear it was an cinch to land. I must say, I never had real trouble landing the Spit with its very narrow gear, but some of my fellow pilots did. In a crosswind it was trickier. We had a lot of landing and take off accidents in Spits while using the short, rutted, muddy, and pot-holed, turf runways on Corsica. I'm sure I speak for the rest of our pilots who flew both Spits and Mustangs in combat. The Spitfire was a beauty to see and to fly. But you wore the Mustang and I'm sure, each of its many pilots felt it was personally tailored. The Mustang was another step up into a magical realm of power, speed and freedom of handling in a fighter.

I recently enjoyed a talk by General Chuck Yeager who, has done about everything imaginable with the widest variety of hot airplanes. This included becoming the first pilot to fly faster than the speed of sound. The general, at one point in his remarks, was extolling the virtues of the Mustang, the plane in which he'd become a World War II Ace. He summed up the praises noting the Mustang's tremendous range advantage and adding something like, " ... and what you could do in a Spitfire for two hours you could continue doing in a Mustang all day."

Thank God! for the Brits, North American and Rosie the Riveter for their roles in the development and mass-production of both great fighters. They bore one naive, mass-produced American pilot safely and even somewhat confidently through the world's biggest and most spectacular air show.

Naturally, I was always grateful and proud to have served my country. That relatively short time in my life will always be of utmost significance to me. But in time I've realized how relatively insignificant that service was to the total scheme of things. My 82 years crossed paths of many people from varied backgrounds who just wouldn't quit trying to make life a little better for others. So, as far as combat service goes, accolades should be limited to those blessed youngsters who gave the ultimate or who were rendered seriously incapacitated ... and maybe to a few others who, on land, sea and air, continue to selflessly heed the cry, "What have you done lately for mankind?"

Epilog

What became of the rest of my life? Perhaps, my headstone could read,

"Had a Rather Unremarkable But Jolly Good Life. Bless All You Contributors."

After a slow readjustment to peacetime and a somewhat clumsy search for a new career, doing it my way has luckily proven warmly rewarding, and there's hardly time enough left for too much to go wrong. My early post-war years were clouded with thoughts like,

There's nothing I could aim for that would be as satisfying as that of a World War II fighter pilot. I was a twenty-one-year-old somebody then, with an exciting, respected and good paying job!

I obviously needed to get past that hang-up. I did but it took some time.

I kept food on the table selling real estate for most of 1946. Then I decided it was time to finish college and back I went to U.C. Santa Barbara on the GI Bill. This and part-time jobs kept my family and me alive, generated a baccalaureate degree, and a couple of years of post graduate studies. I planned on getting a doctoral degree in Clinical Psychology but my GI Bill expired as did bank account and my academic fervor.

While pursuing grad studies I had earned California teaching credentials in three fields and in the late summer of 1951 I grabbed a last minute teaching offer at a junior high school. The job was rewarding in many ways, but a living wage for a family of four wasn't one of them. Moonlighting on a second job became necessary. I certainly hadn't been an outstanding provider. Compounding this problem, my wife Jo, had been raised in a family headed up by one. Still, it was a surprise and shock when she rather abruptly chose to move outward and upward and I wound up a bachelor father with two elementary age kids.

After a few years I found myself teaching in a school administrative environment to which I couldn't adjust. I took what I considered to be an interim job at the Port Hueneme Naval Base in Oxnard, California. This was a management trainee position for which I had been selected through a civil service exam. Never thought I'd be doing anything of this nature but found the work challenging. Within a few years I was promoted to supervisor of the activity's management engineering office ... and became happier job-wise and grocery-wise. My limited job success allowed me the option of passing up some promising job offers elsewhere. One, which was particularly painful to decline, was an opportunity to resume active military duty in the U.S. Air Force. Trouble was, I simply couldn't bring myself to uproot my kids who were clearly doing too well, as situated.

My simple, but 24 hour-per-day working parent life, was on kind of a roll. I began playing tennis regularly and in the late-fifties won a tri-counties open tennis tournament. In 1959 I competed for a nationally advertised job at the nearby Naval Civil Engineering Laboratory. The job was administrative officer and comptroller and when I landed that, I was more surprised and pleased than when I first successfully soloed the Stearman up and away and back down on the grass in 1942.

The lab's mission was research, development and testing of a vast array of military related civil engineering needs including ship to shore systems and equipment. The job was an adventure, a continuing challenge and a constant learning experience. The lab's professional personnel included brilliant and dedicated scientists and engineers of a wide range of disciplines. Their duties took them from the Antarctic to Nome and from Europe through the Pacific basin to Asia. It even included some wide-ranging and exciting temporary duty for me. But, my basic job was my kind of work and kept me challenged until my retirement in the nineteen eighties.

My ultimate reward from all this however, came early on and perfectly packaged. In 1961 one Lois Presnell, who was hired as secretary to the laboratory's commanding officer, charmed me and ultimately became my wife. We added another boy and girl, Mark and Kim, to round out the family. Lois lovingly, diplomatically and patiently established her rightful place in the home. She and daughter Nancy became instant friends and although son John took a little longer, Lois' and his relationship grew ever stronger through the years. John explains to others, today, "Lois is for real. She's a straight shooter." No second-time-around guy, like me, deserves to be so lucky as to have an attractive straight shooter for a mate.

Besides enjoying a satisfying job and enviable home life, I managed to do a few civic things along the way. For many years I served as a Parks and Recreation Commissioner, City of Oxnard. Additionally, I was elected to serve, for several terms, an elected member of the board of directors of the local Federal Credit Union. I was also long-time president of my local municipal tennis club and later a board member of a private tennis club. In later years my church parish trusted me as a trustee. But, my most gratifying church duty continues to be that of singing in its magnificent choir. While not strictly civic, I did complete 21 years in the United States Air Force Reserve. While on short active duty assignments I participated in some rewarding management engineering studies, even managed to enjoy a little jet time and retired as a Lt. Colonel. *En route*, I almost was denied that final reserve duty milestone due to recurring problems from my back injury. The Air Force did drop me from flying duty, early on in my reserve training

As for tennis, I frequently tell friends, "I've created a monster" It was one that enveloped most of the family. Sons, John and Mark, are both tennis professionals and daughter Kim, a strong player, scuba diver, skier, teacher, equestrian and mother. Tennis even trapped Lois who became surprisingly talented with a racket and has given me a built-in hitting partner at home and abroad. As to poetic justice, when I retired from my civilian job, I was finally ensnared in my own net. At a local municipal club and later at a private club I opened tennis pro shops. I operated these businesses for almost two decades. I didn't make much money but found daily retirement joy in the environment.

Lois has accompanied me on the rewarding, revisits to some of my war-time haunts abroad. In 1981 we enjoyed a unique trip to Calvi, Corsica. The Napoleon Bonaparte Hotel was still there, with its bath-less room amenities. It had been commandeered for our 4th Squadron pilot's bed and breakfast, lunch, dinner and bar. Retracing my footsteps through Calvi, my eyes moistened as I seemed to hear children's voices outside a small church. This was a spot where forty years before, local Corsican kids had gathered with their padre and sang us "Home On The Range."

There were more tweaked emotions as I found a small curio shop still run by the same man and wife as in 1943-44. At my insistence, our travel companion, French speaking Heather Campbell, inquired if the couple recalled a Christmas 1943 children's party. It had been one which we pilots arranged for the parish children. Startled, the two rushed from behind their counter with open arms. These shopkeepers had helped with the children's party and remembered me. They were well on in years, at this reunion and it became a magic moment for us all.

As you might guess, our grass runways on Calvi's outskirts had long-since reverted to pastures. Come to think of it, they were just pastures when we flew out of them in World War II. I scanned the northbound pasture and my thoughts drifted.

It's is early January, 1944 I was pushing the Spitfire Mark V throttle gently to the "wall," ... Bumping down the rutted field ... smoothly lifting and raising the gear. I'm tucked in tight to Smitty's wing and climbing. Oh boy ... finally ... this is it ... my first combat mission ... Only just the two of us? We're to do a little scouting from the Savona, Italy area, southwest along the Italian/French Riviera Coast. We are to attack targets of opportunity, or pinpoint them for subsequent patrols. Hope targets of opportunity doesn't include a sky full of enemy fighters. The mission details seem a little vague ... maybe that's normal. Would I do the right thing? Would Smitty? What would we run into? Would we both get back? If I go down and live, wonder if these clothes are appropriate ... for escape? ... Capture?... Damn! Smitty's pushing his nose right down over the water ... Ocean spray on my wind screen ... It's OK! ... Enemy radar screen will be worse.

Reality snapped back in and I pointed out to Lois the majestic, medieval Calvi Citadel guarding the harbor. It hadn't changed noticeably, since '44, nor for centuries before that.

Sadly, my most dominating memories were of the thirteen comrade pilots who came to rest somewhere beyond Calvi's shores, never to revisit this otherwise unforgettable land ... or, more tragically, never their own. During roughly four months of flying Spits from Calvi, we lost about two-thirds of our pilots. Only ten of the original 4th Squadron roll call of 29 pilots answered up as we transitioned to P–51 Mustangs. At war's end, six of the total of nineteen lost were safely repatriated. "Bless 'em all, the long and the short and the tall ..."

Though I was never stationed in England during WWII, Lois and I were delighted with WWII memory lane tour there in summer of 2002. This was a trip guaranteed to whet the appetite of any World War II airplane buff or nostalgia seeker. A happy surprise for me was finding that, after sixty years, British people unfailingly remain captivated by their legendary Battle of Britain. This was the critical engagement, of course, which brought world fame to the Spitfire and its pilots, inflicted the first major victory over the previously invincible Luftwaffe and saved England. As a beginning college freshman in 1940 America, I had marveled at the great victory and the courageous RAF pilots who scored it. Here in 2002 among the indomitable, grateful British I was made to feel praiseworthy merely because I once flew combat in a Spitfire.

And the Brits aren't letting anyone forget the epoch. There are shrines to the battle maintained in London and throughout the country. There are vast and impressive memorials to the American and British air armadas whose dozens of airfields subsequently blanketed rural England. These were the forces that finally devastated Nazi Germany's war-making machine. Here, then, is the setting for Lois' and my "Tour d' Wartime Britain." I'll only mention some highlights. But, I do sincerely hope it will inspire others to share my virtual step back in time and to tour it all.

The British War Museum in London has illuminating and comprehensive historical displays and artifacts spanning ancient to modern warfare. Its World War II coverage is especially dramatic. I barely scratched the surface in seven hours.

The RAF Uxbridge Station, just outside of London, maintains the devilishly deep underground rooms from which British defensive air operations were controlled. One may sit in Winston Churchill's balcony chair overlooking the central control room. Covering much of the control room floor is a large, perhaps twenty by eight foot, table. It's top is a map of England showing RAF fighter bases and other critical locations. This tabled plotting board is surrounded by several RAF women (manikins today) constantly updating a portrayal of the battle situation. The status of every fighter squadron is dynamically maintained with lighted indicators on the wall behind. The center was the hub of command battle communications for the nation and networked with many satellite centers and radar sites. It must have been gut-wrenching for Churchill to have been so intimately involved in the battle process and progress while the fate of his nation hung in the balance.

The RAF Museum at Hendon handsomely displays its finely restored military airplanes spanning the time from RAF birth in the pre-World War I days to the present. World War I Sopwiths and SE–5 fighters and enemy Fokker D–7s and Albatrosses are there. Naturally, World War II Spitfires and Hurricanes and some of their fighter and bomber adversaries are displayed. Animated and speaking manikins in wartime settings, as well as unique film of the times, kind of wraps you up in a rewind. Suddenly, you're a part of the rerun. Likewise the recently completed American Air Museum in England is magnificent.

No Biz Like Air Show Biz

But the climactic event of the tour was the Flying Legends Air Show at Duxford. Think I've seen some of the best air shows in the U.S. ... and the best are spectacular. But they can't get much better than this annual heart-pounding extravaganza. The show-stopper at Duxford is its grand finale wherein more than 50 WWII British and American Army and Navy fighters and bombers become airborne. With highly skilled aerobatics and grace, a thundering beehive of Mustangs, Spitfires, Corsairs, Hurricanes, Wildcats and Thunderbolts accompanied by B–17 and Lancaster heavy bombers, and many more, head for the grandstands. Smaller formations of planes keep coming and spelling each other like a magnified fireworks display. The frenzied antics are so well-timed that there are no mishaps! Finally, a sky-full of mesmerizing relics flies a tight formation and, as an encore, disperses in all directions and contortions. As the fighters and bombers began landing, I shared, with the thousands of chairborne viewers, a feeling of gratitude and of exhaustion.

Not far from Duxford, still on the ceiling of the famous Eagle Bar in Cambridge, rests a masterpiece art legacy. It was done and donated by some of the British and American wartime air crews frequenting the place in the forties. It is an outline of a nude lady ... sketched in red lipstick? Contributors, other than the lipstick artist, added their signatures, squadron designations, casual comments, etc. as masterpiece adornment and background. The task must have involved the ascent of a couple of stacked tables and the apprehension of a rare sober airman or two.

Finally, I must not forget the magnificent American Cemetery at Maddingly dedicated to the memory of the 30,000 American airmen who died flying out of the United Kingdom in the second World War. This beautiful spot was donated by a grateful British people as "their own American soil in England" for these revered Americans.

We recently completed what turned out to be a crowning 2004 nostalgia trip to Italy. We had visited Italy twice before but for various reasons never returned to Madna, our World War II Mustang corral on the Adriatic. It had only taken me 60 years. The trip developed while attending the Branson Missouri reunion of the 52nd Group's 5th Squadron "Spitten Kittens" in the fall of 2003.

Our 4th Squadron pilots had dwindled down to a precious few and, in 2002, we had sounded taps on our reunions. So two of us homeless, Jim McCauley and me, had gladly accepted a kind invitation from our 5th Squadron brothers to join in their reunion.

George Angle of the 5th and his lovely wife Jean hosted the reunion. They not only warmly welcomed Jim and me and our wives, but much more. We learned that on several of their overseas outings, the Angles had revisited Madna, Italy. This was home base to our 52nd Group's 2nd, 4th and 5th, Squadron Mustangs from spring 1944 to the European war's end in spring 1945. When they invited us to meet them on a visit to Madna planned for May of 2004, I excitedly affirmed that if I could continue to dodge the obits that long we'd be there. Regretfully, it became necessary for Jim and Katheren McCauley to bow out due to Katheren's health problems.

So in May of 2004 following enviable days in Rome, Pompei, Sorrento and the Isle of Capri, Lois and I began a rental car trek toward Italy's Adriatic coast and Madna. I must mention that we had stayed in Capri an extra day awaiting improved sea conditions to allow us a rowboat adventure into Capri's Blue Grotto.

Now for those not familiar with the Blue Grotto's uniquely stunning reflections flashing off its cavernous interior walls and waters, you must go see for yourselves. Lois reluctantly looked at the climb down from our launch into a rowboat bobbing beside a sheer 100 foot cliff with a small cave opening at the water line and no beach "Honey, you have got to do this," I pleaded, as I dangled a leg out the launch and the oarsman below steadied me. At first

Lois gasped "No way!" Then shockingly alluding to my wartime Grotto dalliance of 1944, " OK! Damned you! No Italian cutie for you now ... You got me along for this ride ... for better or worse ... Ugh!" (As Lois, with the oarsman's and my help, lands on her back on top of me in the bow of the rowboat). We ducked our heads and the oarsman, lying on his back, deftly pulled our boat through the cave opening and into the huge cavern. Lois could relax, as we sat up and in the sudden silence and almost stilled waters to share the rapturous, colorful glitter the Grotto. Our oarsman's voice, inspired and enhanced by the cavern's natural echo chamber, crescendoed in song ... "Oh Solo Mio." Talk about a second time around, romantic moment ... and squandered on an 82-year-old fool!

We drove the lush, hilly, Italian farmlands of south central Italy for the better part of a day. Enroute, we stopped occasionally for a beer, pasta and some sight-seeing through villages, ranging from incredibly ancient to contemporary. Arriving in the late afternoon on the outskirts of Termoli, one of the larger towns along the mid-boot Italian Adriatic, we found no one familiar with our hotel location. We eventually discovered the main drag of old downtown Termoli and a busy Carbinari directing rush hour traffic. Undoubtedly confounding the poor officer in his duties, I, in my best, broken Italian pleaded for directions to our hotel. Soon enough, he realized an international communications breakdown when he saw one ... beckoned me toward his parked police car and led us on a short but twisted route to our hotel on the beach ... Talk about Italian hospitality.

Awaiting us in the hotel bar were George and Jean Angle, and their accompanying 5th Squadron friends, Dwaine (Bird Dog) Franklin and his wife, Grace. George had arrived for 5th Squadron pilot duty at Madna in the fall of 1944. After almost eighteen months in an around the Med. I had been on my way back to the U.S. and thus George's and my paths hadn't crossed over there. Bird Dog had joined the 5th as all three of the 52nd Group Squadrons were bidding farewell Spitfires and howdy Mustangs, and poised to move to Madna. Bird Dog was one of that select cadre of pilots honored as an Ace.

Also present were Giusseppi Marini of Campomarino, a picturesque Italian village and the closest community of any size to our Madna airfield. Giusseppi and the Angles had met on previous Angle trips to Italy and continued to correspond. Giusseppi had done a bushel of research on the beehive of allied bomber and fighter airfields surrounding the area and specifically Madna. Giusseppi is an impressive guy and recognized local WWII historian and lecturer. Giusseppi is so ambitious he would like to re-fashion a portion of our Madna as a local memorial. It would not surprise me to see Giusseppi, the Angles and the people of Campomarino join in a remake of the WWII Madna area, with Mustangs and all, as a shrine to its glory days.

There at our arrival too, was Framicio, an affable, well educated a young man, George and Jean's driver and owner of a chauffeur business. Framicio, a native Italian, was a consummate interpreter and spoke well-constructed English. This attribute turned out to be invaluable in this less traveled, Adriatic side of the Italian peninsula.

After our long drive, Lois and I were ready at 5 p.m. to peek under the yardarm for a relaxing cocktail and dinner. George and Duaine, however, were raring to visit Madna and away we soberly sped. Our original presence of 60 years ago, in what was an air base plunked in a wheatfield, was now camouflaged by the addition of new vegetation and absence of an original runway. But, the area is still rural, and unlike so much of our Southern California it wasn't paved over with the trappings of exploding civilization and development. In fact, a narrow, gravel farm road stretches directly down the path of what once was our 4,000 feet of steel-matted runway.

The wheatfield is now mostly olive trees and a few vineyards. Other pre-fab facilities and equipment, common to fighter plane and pilot maintenance have long vanished. Strewn along both sides of the road and into the olive orchards were remains of the heavy gauge gravel used as a soil stabilizer for the runway matting. Some of the matting is yet in use for various purposes in and around farmyards. One rectangular piece of matting was attached to a tractor rig, apparently as a grading device.

George Angle, Dwain "Bird-Dog" Franklin & Author
at 52nd Group Headquarters - 2004
Photo courtesy of Bob McCampbell

· George pointed out and I recognized a pair of almost identical, two story farmhouses, located perhaps a mile a part and not too far from the runway. One was used as our 52nd Group headquarters building, where the pilots of all three squadrons gathered for pre-mission briefings. The other had been home to several of the luckier 5th Squadron pilots such as George Angle and Dwain Franklin. Most of the rest of the pilots, including me, were afforded tents. I did have a rare tree outside of mine. This opened opportunities for luxury amenities like a place to hang towels, a mirror, a GI helmet of heated water and a clothesline. The tree also added a picnic atmosphere where we could sometimes cook a rare meal on a Coleman stove. George and Dwain now tell me they barbecued on their balcony ... talk about the privileged few!

Both the buildings were occupied, at this visit, but George and Giusseppi were able to contact the current residents of the one occupied by 5th Squadron and we all enjoyed an inside tour. George and Dwain found the very rooms which lodged them 60 years earlier. In an annex to their palace was what had been the old 5th Squadron bar. It was full of farm junk. But still cartooned on a plaster wall was the legacy

Author & Ted Bullock at 52nd Group
Headquarters - 1944
Photo courtesy of Bob McCampbell

of a pilot artist. It was a drawing of the famous ubiquitous, mythical GI character, Kilroy in two poses ... both drunken. At least Herman didn't take this masterpiece along with the rest of the art he stole from the Louvre in Paris.

We were unable to tour the inside of the headquarters building. We did take some 2004 snaps to compare with a 1944 photo of Abdul Bullock and me posing in front of the headquarters a few days before shipping out to the States. Some window and balcony remodeling had occurred in these few sixty years.

On the menu for the following day, we were surprised to find that Giusseppi had arranged for the city council of Campomarino to honor the three of us former liberators at a special meeting. One must realize that when I had arrived in North Africa and even later in Sicily, the Italians had been a part of the Axis powers and as such they were our enemy. How that relationship changed is a subject for another memoir much longer than this one. Allow me a short bit of background.

The Italian people had suffered under the twenty-year yoke of their dictator, Benito Mussolini. As an ally of Germany's dictator, Adolph Hitler, Mussolini had developed a sizable and apparently formidable army, navy and air force. Unfortunately for Benito, his armed forces seemed to account themselves as more lovers than fighters, especially when it came to having much heart to fight the Americans. Compounding that disadvantage they never got along too well with their fellows in arms, the Nazi forces. The situation must have made Mussolini, "Il Duce," (his

Lois & Bob at 52nd Group Headquarters - 2004
Photo courtesy of Bob McCampbell

self-styled title) apoplectic as we and the Brits captured tens of thousands of his soldiers in North Africa, overran Sicily, followed by British and American landings in Southern Italy.

As might have been expected, a military coup erupted, ousting Il Duce and replacing him with Italy's top soldier, General Bagdolio. The general took no time before flying down to Palermo, Sicily and surrendering Italy to the Allies. It took place at our Spitfire base in mid-summer of 1943. Our squadron had been ordered to stand down. My buddies and I stood goggle-eyed watching a prearranged escort of Allied and Italian fighters covering an Italian tri-motor transport as it landed on our base. We were even more dazzled when we watched as Italian brass dismounted the transport, paraded toward awaiting Allied brass ... and as General Bagdolio passed his sword and his country over to our side. We thought the war was over ... It took, as you know, almost two more hard-fought years before it really happened. Of course the Germans were well-entrenched in Italy at the time and became heavily reinforced. The Italian people thus became an occupied people and eventually happier than ever to welcome the advancing Americans.

So, we were among friends in 1943 Italy. As typified by the Campomarino city council gesture, we certainly found amicability still alive and well in 2004. Not clearly understanding what was in store for us at the council meeting, we followed Giusseppi into council chambers crowded with Campomarino townspeople, high school student leaders, and the local Termoli Press. Up front, George, Dwaine and I were seated side by side, at a long speaker table facing the audience. Decorated name cards and bottled waters marked our places. Surely I wasn't destined to speak that much. Framicio was seated behind us as an interpreter and what a masterful job he was to perform. At my right sat Giusseppi's wife, Professor Margherita Recchia, a respected local educator. I noted her name plate identified her as "Maderatore." Beyond her sat the mayor, the high school principal and other local dignitaries.

The entire program was conducted in Italian with Framicio whispering enough English to keep us in the loop. Margharita introduced us with some laudatory preliminaries, greeted by cheers and applause. She followed with explanations of the honorarium format and a meeting outline.

A Campomarino High School girls quartet performed some Andrews Sisters WWII songs and some universal kids-style rock tunes. After more recognition from others at our table, Margharita opened a question and answer period to be directed our way. The townspeople and a few high school students asked some good questions about the war and our participation. They were also interested in our daily lives there and our memories of Campomarino. One attractive young woman asked, "Did you ever think much about women?" To which Duaine replied, hesitatingly, "I was trying to think of a time when we didn't." I should note that we three honorees were apparently the oldest members of the gathering. We did find one man almost as old as we, who had been employed as a teenager to build our runway in '44, but, alas, no old girlfriends showed up.

Giusseppi then presented a masterfully organized and professionally delivered slide show summary of World War II and Italy's involvement. He continued with detailed discussion and illustration of the famous complex of nearby Allied airfields in Campomarino's 1944 and 1945 backyard. He concluded with specifics about our Madna airfield. He kindly included some personal background and old slide photos of each of us and our airplanes.

The Campomarino City Council presented us each with an honorary resolution on behalf of the city, The daily *Nuovo Molise* (Termoli Newspaper) published our pictures and called us heroes and the high school students asked for our autographs. In complete hu-

TERMOLI-LITORALE

Campomarino - Il rientro degli aviatori dopo 60 anni

Tre eroi tornano alla «base»
E la Storia diventa più ricca

Giusseppi Marini of Campomarino
organizes a tribute to three American fighter pilots
Photo courtesy of Bob McCampbell

mility I can only say many thanks to a warm and compassionate people.

As Lois and I drove away and said good-bye to our Campomarino *Paisanos*, I took a last look at what used to be the runway at Madna.

> *In a flash, two thirds of a mile of steel runway matting unfurled over its small road replacement. Nearby, my old tent arose in a wheatfield next to lonely tree. In no time, all sorts of tents, sheds and people were appearing and everyone hurriedly scurrying about ... In and out of mess lines, the HQ building, and fully loaded jeeps moving toward the flight line. My God! There's got to be more than fifty yellow-tailed Mustangs, gathered in three separate bunches along*

both sides of the runway. Yep, there's The 4ᵗʰ
Squadron WD's ... can't pick out mine from here.
"Hey Jimmy! They givin you a bad time bout
your snoring, up in Headquarters?" "Got to say
I don't miss it in the tent." "Hi Trib! I'll join you
for breakfast. Tyler taking the squadron today?
Hey Abdul! Want to join Trib and me at the
beach today?" Oh Lord, I was gonna tell pappy
he could wash off that dirty old Lake Okeebogee
water in the Adriatic today ... How could I?...
Pap didn't make it back yesterday. I'm strapped
in ol' WD-D, Fitz is flying wing and right behind
me. There goes Tim Tyler off. Here we go Tackle
Yellow. It's gonna be another butbustin five
hours of bladder-straining glory. The Mustang's
gotta be the greatest ... but it stays up too long.
What am I bitchin about? ... Might have been in
the trenches freezin my butt off all night.

"Bob," Lois reminds, "Time to hit the
Autostrada."

So here I am, in my eighties, with few regrets
other than wondering what I want to be when I grow
up. I passed through a glorious youthful phase as an
average fighter pilot with, perhaps, more exciting than
average experiences. Certainly, I had better than average luck. Finally, if the reward of love is any goal in life
I must have received more than my share.

Occasionally, I try a mental camcorder shot of
myself as a reasonably confident 21-year-old, calmly
leading a fighter squadron into combat against a formidable enemy. But, there goes the image again, fading away in the viewfinder.

Index

Symbols

A

X

Y

Z

SECONDWIND
BOOKWORKS

Quick Order Form

Telephone orders: Call 805-650-6998
Internet orders: www.secondwindbookworks.com
Postal orders: send this form with your check
or credit card information to:

SecondWind BookWorks
1198 Navigator Drive, #65
Ventura, CA 93001

Please send the following books. I understand
that I may return any of them for a full refund
- for any reason, no questions asked.

Ordinary Guy, Extraordinary Times   **$18.95**

Qty.	X_____
Sub-Total	$_____
Tax (CA only)	$_____
Shipping	$_____
Grand Total	$_____

Credit Card orders:
Card: (check one)   □ MasterCard   □ Visa
Card number :_____
Name on Card: _____
Expiration Date: _____ (month) _____ (year)
Security Code: _____ (3 digits from the back of card)

Send to:
Name:_____
Address:_____
City:_____ State:_____ Zip:_____
Telephone:_____E-mail:_____

Sales Tax: Please add 7.25% for products shipped to
California addresses. ($1.30 for each book)
Shipping: U.S.: Add $4.00 for first book and $2.00 for
each additional book. International: Add $9.00 for first
book and $5.00 for each additional book.

Also Available from
SecondWind BookWorks

Visit us on the web at
www.secondwindbookworks.com

Groundbreaking, Encouraging, Compassionate!

The Alzheimer's Dialogues are not lectures.
They are part talk show, part seminar, part support group.

In these interactive and honest presentations,
Nancy Graham's groundbreaking role gives voice to caregivers everywhere.
Nancy expresses the feelings and fears family members experience
when facing a loved one's descent into dementia.
Her brave truth-telling gives the audience permission
to process their own emotions
and to ask the questions they must have answered.

Sherril Bover is there to answer questions and to
bring encouragement and compassion.
As the calm, empathetic friend with experience in caregiving,
Sherril communicates hope and understanding and lets caregivers know
that they are not alone in the Alzheimer's journey.

The Alzheimer's Dialogues are presented in four sessions:
The Basics
Exploring the Elements of Dementia
Communication
Moving from Honesty to Mercy in the New Language of Alzheimer's
Behavior
The Embarrassing, the Heartbreaking and the Downright Dangerous
Self Care
Finding Serenity in Acceptance

The two-CD set includes all four sessions
and a booklet of vital information

"A joy to the listener!"
"Difficult information presented in a caring way."

Praise for The Alzheimer's Dialogues

*"In the session on communication,
I totally got it! I understand now why our conversations
are so weird between my husband and me."*

*"Difficult issues presented in a caring way!
Honesty! Hope!"*

*"Could you please have more
Dialogues like these?"*

*"Participants have consistently raved about The
Alzheimer's Dialogues and expressed
great appreciation for them. As education coordinator,
I am extremely proud to offer a program for family caregivers
that not only impart valuable information,
but also touches the heart so deeply."*

Linda Sharp, Education Coordinator, Alzheimer's Association

*"This excellent series of pertinent caregiving issues
offers practical techniques, interaction and
communication about real situations in a safe,
supportive setting. A must for caregivers!"*

Fran McNeill, Director of Family Services, Alzheimer's Association

**Visit us on the web at
*www.secondwindbookworks.com***

Quick Order Form

Telephone orders: Call 805-650-6998
Internet orders: www.secondwindbookworks.com
Postal orders: send this form with your check
or credit card information to:

SecondWind BookWorks
1198 Navigator Drive, #65
Ventura, CA 93001

Please send the following. I understand that I
may return any of them for a full refund - for
any reason, no questions asked.

The Alzheimer's Dialogues   *$39.95*

Qty.	X_____
Sub-Total	$_____
Tax (CA only)	$_____
Shipping	$_____
Grand Total	$_____

Credit Card orders:

Card: (check one)   □ MasterCard   □ Visa
Card number :_____
Name on Card: _____
Expiration Date: _____ (month) _____ (year)
Security Code: _____ (3 digits from the back of card)

Send to:

Name:_____
Address:_____
City:_____ State:_____ Zip:_____
Telephone:_____E-mail:_____

Sales Tax: Please add 7.25% for products shipped to
California addresses. ($2.90 for each)
Shipping: U.S.: Add $4.00 for first CD set and $2.00 for
each additional set. International: Add $9.00 for first CD
set and $5.00 for each additional set.

SECONDWIND
BOOKWORKS

Visit us on the web at
www.secondwindbookworks.com